How an Ivy League College

Decides on Admissions

HOW AN
IVY LEAGUE COLLEGE
DECIDES
ON ADMISSIONS

Katharine T. Kinkead

W · W · NORTON & COMPANY · INC · *New York*

INTRODUCTION

THE following story of the operations of the Yale College admissions office in its year-long task of choosing a freshman class is the specific study of how the students who completed their first year in June, 1961, at that university were selected. The candidates facing the committee decisions at New Haven will for a good many Mays hereafter encounter much the same process. For unless major innovations not now anticipated are introduced, the admissions procedure, with its intricate weighing of youthful achievements and personalities, with its pondering of figures and its preoccupation with numbers, will remain necessarily as delicately complex for a good many years to come. The many letters from admissions directors of colleges and universities throughout the country which greeted the Yale story when it appeared in a shorter version as "The Brightest Ever" in *The New Yorker* magazine seem to indicate that the general process used at New Haven is similar to that of most institutions today enjoying the painful blessings of being truly selective. These may be said principally to comprise, of course, the remaining Ivy League schools and those other prestigious, geographically scattered, and often quite contrasting establishments whose application rolls these days normally reveal a press of some three or more aspirants vying for every place.

As this book goes to press, for the first time in almost a decade some of the top colleges report a decline in applications, ranging from ten per cent at Yale to some twenty per cent at Amherst. Most admission heads welcome this drop as evidence that multiple applications are being stemmed a bit and that obviously unqualified candidates, prodded by their college guidance counselors, have taken off their rose-colored glasses and applied elsewhere. This is the case at Yale. There its admission dean, Arthur Howe, Jr., in the throes of tallying up his final figures for the newly admitted freshmen, reports that Yale accepted one hundred fewer candidates this June than last year to obtain its full class, that the same problems were felt even more intensely, that the quality of the applicants was higher than ever, and the task of choosing among them correspondingly more difficult. Not surprisingly, the Freshman Dean's office is again ready to announce the incoming class "The Brightest Ever."

Without perceptibly adding to the staff's burdens, Howe said, the new entrance test required this year by Yale—the one-hour written essay on a subject chosen by the College Board—had given the further insights the committee had hoped into a candidate's character and his ability to organize and set down his thoughts. "The subject of the exam was 'Loyalty,'" added Howe. "We got a fine variety of replies—everything from a six-paragraph eulogy one boy wrote of his dead dog to a six-page attack, bristling with facts, on the House Un-American Affairs Committee."

To a thoughtful outsider, the spectacle of the Yale admissions procedure is a heartening one. For in spite of the hundreds of qualified youngsters applying, Yale's selection remains an individual and personal process. In some quarters the process is contracting to a weighing of figures or symbols of the individual student. There are institutions discouraging for instance, the personal interview. Granted the interview may be an imperfect and sometimes useless means of judging young people, it serves to remind admission men that they are dealing not with Candidate Number 2859 but with a changing, developing human being in the process of rapidly shedding his adolescent skin.

Unfortunately there is a trend today toward judging college candidates from paper data—from the results of multiple-choice tests whose answers are written out in the questions themselves and which permit the elements of personality, of creativity, and of individual talents little chance of showing through—and from school records and teacher resumés pre-digested for admission officers by the secondary-school guidance men. The guidance man, particularly in public high schools, has become an essential part of the educational operation. He is the sifter who decides which children enter the curriculum "tracks" bound for four-year colleges as well as, later, whether they will apply for first, second, or third-rate institutions. He is rarely a teacher himself and occasionally has never been one. His personal knowledge of his charges may extend only to a brief interview in their senior year. Yet without his backing a youngster has little hope of being accepted by a college he wants. In the face of the tides of students bound for college, this situation may be unavoidable, but at least, excellence can be infused into its operation. Communities can see that the guidance departments are staffed by men and women with the education and vision to recommend, for instance, that American phenomenon the late male bloomer (one of whom seems to grace almost every home), as well as the mavericks—the original, the creative, and even the rebellious types. Perhaps one might say especially the rebellious student—the girl or boy, not particularly cherished by the school administration, who dares assert his spunky individuality by getting a low grade in a course given by a dull teacher or in a subject outside his interest while he soars high in the fields where his real talent lies. Otherwise it is not too difficult to imagine a future top college population composed substantially of the successful test-takers and "little twerps" Arthur Howe sometimes has nightmares about.

How an Ivy League College

Decides on Admissions

CHAPTER
ONE

UNDER the heading "United States Colleges and Universities," the current edition of Webster's New Collegiate Dictionary lists the names of over two thousand institutions. Of these, the number offering four-year programs of undergraduate study in the liberal arts and sciences is put by educators at seven hundred and fifty. Last year, these seven hundred and fifty colleges received applications for admittance from some seven hundred and fifty thousand secondary-school students—an alarmingly high figure, since the average college can accommodate nowhere near a thousand freshmen and, in any case, the average applicant is notably unwilling to settle for the average college. Under these circumstances, and because the number of young people who annually try to get into college has nearly doubled since the Second World War, the once fairly placid business of college admissions has lately acquired the dimensions of a sizable industry, some of the jargon of a social science, and a structure like that of a vertically organized labor union. Near the base of the pyramid is a large corps of practitioners of the relatively new profession of college guidance counseling, at least one of whom is now found in every up-and-coming high school and prep school in the country. At the pinnacle of the edifice are the admissions officers of the approximately forty American colleges that, if you are over twenty-five and have not recently had reason to concern yourself with such matters, you will probably think of simply as first-rate schools but that, if you are either trying to get into college or trying to help get somebody else in, you will most likely refer to as "selective," "competitive," or "prestige" institutions. While such usages, prime examples of the new admissions jargon, have their origin in the fact that the forty-odd colleges in question have many more applicants than they can take, much of the popularity of the appellations can be traced to the way they protect a guidance man when he breaks the news to querulous parents that their child will have to be content with admission to what he calls "an excellent little liberal-arts institution," which the parents have never heard of.

There is no definitive and immutable list of the prestige schools, but prominent in the category are, of course, the trio that the guidance men refer to as H.Y.P. (Harvard, Yale, and Princeton), and the other Ivy League universities; such Midwestern educational giants as the Universities of Chicago and Michigan; Stanford and Berkeley, on the West Coast; and, elsewhere, such relatively small but educationally impeccable institutions as Haverford and Wesleyan. Although the competition among girls for admission to the colleges that the guidance-and-admissions people have dubbed the Heavenly Seven (Barnard, Bryn Mawr, Mount Holyoke, Radcliffe, Smith, Vassar, and Wellesley) is just as keen as that among boys headed for correspondingly exalted institutions, by and large it is the struggle to get male offspring into one of the better universities that is more apt to unhinge parents. These days, primary-school teachers have ceased to be particularly surprised by anxious mothers' and fathers' demands to know at once whether their sons are prestige-college material, and by the time a boy is a senior Cub Scout he will, if he *is* prestige-college material, scarcely bat an eye upon being told that he must work hard on his mathematics so that he can qualify for the junior-high-school honors group that feeds into the high-school advanced-math section that feeds into the high-school advanced-placement math program of college-level work. And by the time the youth has reached his junior year of high school, he is totally immersed in the intricacies of college selection, whether he is headed for comparative-literature studies in a prestige college or merely hopes to squeak into one of his guidance man's little liberal-arts institutions. He is exhorted to become "motivated," so that he will work "at the top of his potential," and "to get steamed up about something," because, he is assured, "colleges look for students who can throw themselves into things." As he enters his senior year, if he has any stuff in him at all, he will probably throw himself into a last, frantic sprint for the highest grades he can pull down—that is, provided he can spare the time from the cycle of reading-skill, intelligence, vocational-guidance, and sometimes even personality tests that are being given him to "gauge his strengths and weaknesses," to say nothing of a special examination that is supposed to predict his score on the College Entrance Examination Board tests still ahead of him. In advisers' interviews, assembly lectures by returning alumni, and school-distributed books and pamphlets, he is told how and when to write his first letter to a college, even if it is merely a request for a catalogue; he is instructed in how to dress, act, and talk in interviews with college admissions men; and he is likely to be given from four to six coaching sessions in how to take the College Board tests, which are required for admission to practically all the prestige colleges and to around three hundred others. Throughout this time the candidate is buffeted by rumors: Harvard and Yale admit no one whose college board scores are below 700; Princeton keeps one place open for a flute player; Amherst accepts only valedictorians or geniuses; Swarthmore takes a dim view of applicants who cannot debate in a foreign language; and a certain state institution will give a full scholarship, job, and car to anyone who can kick a football sixty yards. All of these, of course, except perhaps the last, are untrue.

The immediate target of all such effort, analysis, cramming, and prayer is the college admissions officer. This simultaneously harassed and exalted faculty member may have come to his job as a member of the academic staff who has revealed a talent for administration, or he may be a professional guidance expert. In the small, nonprestige colleges, his main worry, even in these days of educational overpopulation, may be that his institution is not attracting enough applicants to enable it to practice any selectivity in putting its student body together—or perhaps even to fill its freshman class. At many of the big state universities, by contrast, the admissions man is not troubled by any dearth of candidates, but he may be troubled by the fact that his school's charter or his state's laws force him to accept most of those who apply, regardless of their qualifications, with the result that his office becomes little more than a filing department. As for the admissions men at the top competitive schools, their duties are so complex and their decisions so crucial that they are now probably the most overworked, overfeared, and overcriticized men in contemporary American education. Of all the pitfalls they face, the most frightening, if not the most likely, is the possibility that they will wreck, or at least seriously cripple, their institutions by admitting far more students than can be accommodated, or by committing the colleges to disburse much more money in scholarships than they can afford. The reason either or both of these nightmarish situations can come to pass is that nowadays terrified secondary-school youngsters apply for as many colleges as they happen to feel like applying for, on the theory that the more applications they put in, the better their chances are for getting into a decent school. Unfortunately, the admissions men very often have no way of discovering how many other colleges each applicant is trying for, nor have they any way of knowing, after they have spent months poring over qualifications and culling their lists, how many of the students they decide to admit actually intend to come to their college, or how many of the brilliant, needy youths whom they attempt to lure with scholarships will rise to the bait. The admissions officer's only way of allowing for what he and his confreres call "ghost" applications is to admit more students than there are places in the freshman class. This in no way protects him from waking up some summer morning, after the books are closed, and discovering that he has acceptances from a freshman class either half as large or twice as large as the school has room for. Since the danger of too many acceptances is greater than that of too few, and since in recent years some prestige colleges have reported receiving up to twelve times as many applications as there are places to be filled (a figure which, in some cases, their rivals claim is padded by mere catalogue requests) the pressure on these institutions to expand their educational and physical facilities has been enormous. A few have done so, but most have decided in favor of very little expansion or none at all, preferring to defend the liberal-arts tradition as they know it, rather than risk diluting the quality of their scholarship or their instruction, or expose their undergraduate programs to the demands for early specialization and even vocational courses which they feel expansion would bring.

Among the schools that have most forthrightly taken this stand is Yale University, whose president, A. Whitney Griswold, said not long ago, "We have no thought of doubling our student body by 1970, or of increasing it arbitrarily by any fixed percentage. On the face of it, this could be taken for an unresponsive, even an 'undemocratic' attitude, and there are voices that counsel us not to mention it, lest it be so interpreted. I think we had better mention it and acknowledge it, for it is exactly what we mean to do." Over most of the past decade, Yale has had a ratio of between three and four well-qualified applicants for every place in its freshman class, whose size is stipulated by the supervisory Yale Corporation and was last raised in 1941, from eight hundred and fifty to a thousand. Since the tide of Yale applicants is now up to almost five boys per vacancy, and since Yale's admissions office has been a leader in trying to solve the problems that arise from such overabundance, I decided around the first of the year to see if I could arrange a series of visits to that office in order to learn how the university goes about making up its freshman class. When I called Arthur Howe, Jr., Yale's Dean of Admissions, he was agreeable to my plan, if hardly enthusiastic about it. "It's practically impossible for us to say anything about admissions these days without sounding either smug or obscure," he said. "From time to time a college may get out of balance and have special needs or problems that are temporarily reflected in its admission policy. But we think we're in fairly good shape here now. At least, every year the Freshman Dean's office announces that the new class is the brightest ever. And at the moment we're hunting for boys who will make next year's even brighter." He granted me the appointments I asked for, after jocularly inquiring whether I was sure I wasn't the mother or sister of any current Yale applicants, and also after obtaining my promise both to safeguard the identities of any boys I might write about and to read as many as possible of the folders in which Yale files its extensive information on all those who apply. "It's difficult to understand what we're up against unless you do a good bit of folder reading," he said. He went on to tell me that, because of university rules, I would not be permitted to attend the actual admissions-committee meetings, in late April and early May, at which the new Yale men are chosen, but that he would be glad to let me sit in with the committee before it began its closed sessions. Having undertaken to abide by his conditions, I made an appointment with him for the following week.

CHAPTER

TWO

THE Yale admissions office is in Welch Hall, one of a row of aging reddish-brown stone structures along the east side of the Old Campus Quadrangle, which was the original, eighteenth-century site of the college, and most of whose buildings are now used as freshman dormitories. Opposite it, across the wide expanse of the town green with its three historic churches neat in a row, Yale meets the city of New Haven. Back to the west and up to the north lie the University's many blocks of buildings, quadrangles, inner courtyards and stone archways in colonial, neo-gothic or contemporary architecture.

On that late winter morning as I walked across the flagstones and under the great elms of the Old Campus to keep my appointment with Mr. Howe, the blend of youth and age, of heady activity and monastic reflection which is the peculiar aura of a New England college, was apparent. Bicycles leaned against the ivy-covered walls of the dormitories and of Connecticut Hall, the Georgian building that was Yale's first permanent structure. Before the latter the statue of its onetime resident Nathan Hale, of the class of 1773, stood green-stained in the thin winter sun.

In Welch Hall I entered a pleasantly furnished reception room. Several youths, obviously candidates for admission, sat about, some of them elaborately absorbed in magazines or university booklets, others making no attempt to conceal their apprehension over the coming interviews with members of Howe's staff. The more nervous boys swung their crossed legs, tapped their feet, or drummed on the chair arms, and watched every movement in an adjacent corridor, onto which a number of small offices opened. Also in the reception room, but sitting carefully apart from the boys, were several adults—parents, I deduced from the intent and proprietary way each of them was watching a particular youngster. A tall, slim, dark-haired young woman, who was identified by a card on her desk as Miss Barbara Bonnardi, presided over this jumpy assemblage. When I gave her my name, she told me that Mr. Howe would see me in a moment, offered me a booklet called "An Introduction to Yale," and beckoned me to a chair.

Looking through the booklet, I discovered, among other things, that Yale now has just under eight thousand students, of whom about four thousand are undergraduates, and that, out of the possibility of over fifty different majors, five out of six students select those in the liberal arts and sciences and the other sixth in engineering. More than sixty-five per cent of the undergraduates ultimately go on to some sort of advanced study. (In the nineteen-twenties, when a prominent Yale alumnus expressed the prevailing American opinion that graduate students were men who did not know enough to go home when the party was over, the figure was less than twenty per cent.) After the freshman year, I read, Yale undergraduates live in residential colleges of around three hundred members, each built about a quadrangle, with its own dining hall, recreation rooms, library, athletic teams, chapel, newspaper, visiting lecturers, Master in residence, and honorary and faculty fellows—an arrangement which Yale, along with a few other top institutions, finds an answer to the problem of maintaining the advantages of intimate college life with the intellectual resources of a university.

As I was digesting these facts, a young man with a faculty look about him entered the room from the corridor and read a name from a slip of paper. "John!" one of the mothers whispered stridently to a boy across the room, who was huddled over a magazine. "You are being called!" John leaped wildly to his feet, caught his heel in the base of a coat rack beside his chair, and was enveloped in a mass of swaying garments. The interviewer helped him extricate himself and, with a light remark and a nice degree of friendly amusement, did what he could to restore the youth's aplomb. Then, after chatting a bit with John's mother, he led the boy off down the corridor. Miss Bonnardi now announced that Mr. Howe would see me, and I followed her past offices that emanated a constrained conversational murmur, above which momentarily rose a young male voice asserting loudly, "Yes, sir. Shakespeare, sir."

As Dean of Admissions, and Director of Yale's Office of Admissions and Freshman Scholarships, Howe also supervises Yale's Office of Counseling and Placement, its Office of Educational Research, and its Financial Aids Office, and is, in addition, a member of the powerful Course of Study Committee of Yale College, which initiates all curriculum changes. In view of these numerous and weighty responsibilities of his, I was a trifle surprised to be greeted by a tall, thoughtful-looking man, in dark-framed glasses, who clearly couldn't be much over forty. I learned that Howe had gone to Hotchkiss, and had entered Yale with the class of 1943, which he had left during the Second World War to become an American Field Service officer in the Middle East, North Africa, and Italy. After the war, he had returned to Yale to get his degree, then had taught at Hotchkiss for a while, left there to study for a year at Oxford, and finally come back to Yale, where he served as Assistant Freshman Dean until, in 1955, he acquired his present multiple jobs.

"Sometimes I'm not sure whether I'm doing admissions work or public relations," Howe said. "Many people tend to think that the admissions office *is* the university, and they drop in from all over the world just to see us or to tell us about a nephew or a neighbor's boy. No matter what we do, we're almost certain to be unsuccessful as far as public relations go. For one thing, we hurt more people than we can ever please. And because we must constantly make judgments and predictions about the characters and future contributions of human beings, we make mistakes. Just the same, I hope the day will never come when we think we can measure each individual's potential value precisely. We would probably, in that case, operate under a quota system whereby we would decide how many of each kind of student would make the ideal Yale class, and assign each candidate a rating in a particular category. That I hope we never do."

Initially, Howe said, his biggest problem had been to learn how to live from day to day with an unusually large assortment of conflicting pressures—from secondary schools, from parents, from alumni, from the Yale faculty, and also from his own sympathies. "Of course, none of these things would worry me so much if we didn't have such a glut of applications," he went on. "But there is a bright side even to that. For one thing, the secondary schools have had to raise their scholastic standards, and, for another, we can now pick and choose very carefully among the candidates."

He gave me a brief outline of how the methods of judging a boy's fitness for admission to Yale have changed over the past century. "A hundred years ago," he said, "some professor would line up the applicants outside his study door, admit them one by one, put them through a stiff oral exam in Latin or Greek, and tell them to come back the next day for his decision—a method that some of our faculty members think would still work as well as any that the modern experts have concocted." Around the turn of the century, he continued, when public high schools had sprung up all over America, producing a vast increase in college applications, the colleges needed more exact ways of evaluating the applicants' academic records and abilities. As one means to this end, a system was evolved of giving units of credit for secondary-school work based on so many classroom minutes spent so many times a week on a subject. Then in 1900 a group of Eastern universities jointly set up the College Entrance Examination Board, which soon devised the first of a fearsome series of written tests. Until the Second World War, the secondary-school seniors taking College Board exams were required to display their knowledge of the subjects concerned by writing encyclopedic essays or solving complex problems. "By the end of the war," Howe said, "both the system of high-school credits and the essay-type exams had fallen into disuse—the former because it's obviously unfair to give equal credits in English to a boy who has studied Aeschylus and Faulkner at an academically excellent school and a boy who has read not much more than 'Silas Marner' at Cross Forks High. And the old College Board exams were abandoned partly because it was impossible to grade them uniformly—the Cross Forks High boy might write a more brilliant essay than the other kid but get a lower mark, depending on who graded the paper. Also, the avalanche of applicants was just too much for those doing the grading. So now we evaluate secondary-school studies on the basis of the whole pattern of work a student has done in essential subjects, and we examine the youngsters by means of multiple-choice College Boards tests, which are graded by machines."

This kind of examination, I learned, is often called an "objective test" because it requires the student to identify the correct answer to a question from among several suggested answers rather than to make up his own. "Ordinarily, in his senior year of high school," Howe continued, "every boy applying for Yale takes the College Board scholastic aptitude test, a three-hour test in two sections, measuring his general verbal and mathematical ability, and then three one-hour College Board achievement tests, covering what he has learned in three of his high school subjects—usually English, social studies or a foreign language, and one of the sciences. The tests are graded on a scale of 200 to 800 points. 475 is the average nation-wide score of all students taking the test."

In 1946, Howe went on, with entrance requirements less hidebound, and the government paying the veterans' way through college, Yale, for the first time in its history, had about twice as many fully qualified applicants as it could admit. That year, by special dispensation of the Yale Corporation, it matriculated fourteen hundred and fifty boys—four hundred and fifty more than the normal limit. By 1950, the veterans had been fairly well taken care of, but new pressures had been building up as Yale encouraged, and received, applications from boys whose geographical, social, or economic backgrounds might in the past have kept them away. That same year, the College Entrance Examination Board dropped its requirement that applicants list their first, second, and third choice of college on their test forms, and the seams burst open. The waiving of this rule, at the request of secondary-school authorities who felt that in many cases a college might be prejudiced against a youngster who did not make it his first choice, resulted in floods of ghost applications, which have not been fully stemmed to this day, despite the introduction of a ten-dollar application fee and secondary-school guidance men's efforts to keep their charges' applications to a maximum of three.

"Before that," Howe said, "an H.Y.P. admissions officer could count on acceptances from ninety-five per cent of the applicants chosen, could assume that fifty of these would withdraw over the summer, for one reason or another, and then could sit back and enjoy himself. Now we must accept fifteen hundred candidates to get the thousand we want, and offer about a hundred thousand dollars more than our available funds to produce the scholarship acceptances we count on. The real headache, of course, is picking the right fifteen hundred boys. That figure, by the way, includes about four hundred and fifty boys who are offered scholarships and about three hundred boys who have applied for scholarships but are granted admission without the scholarships. There's always a chance that such a boy will pull a prosperous grandmother out of a closet somewhere, and anyway, even if he has lost out to someone else on a scholarship, we don't want to turn him down entirely just because his father happens to be poor. We'd like to have him here if he can manage it financially. Usually it turns out that about seventy such boys do decide they can.

"It's easy enough," Howe went on, "to admit the obviously good prospects and reject the obviously weak ones, as it was in the past, but today over eighty-five per cent of our candidates are what we would have considered *fully* qualified twenty-five years ago. In those days, the mean score on the C.E.E.B. scholastic-aptitude test for the entering freshman class was 540, on a scale of 200 to 800 points, which meant that the average Yale student then stood ahead of sixty of every hundred students taking the test. Today our freshmen average 647 in the verbal test and 667 in the mathematics— a score which puts them ahead of about 90 out of every 100 students taking the test. And the figure goes up every year.

Yet the tests aren't everything. No test ever devised can be regarded as a fully reliable index to *general* intelligence. But the College Boards, particularly the aptitude tests, fulfill their intended function of measuring, approximately of course, the *developed* academic ability without which no boy can succeed at Yale or any other good college. The aptitude test does not have the other characteristic which, traditionally, a good academic test should have—it can't be used as a teaching device nor does it encourage any desirable learning pattern. And that's the source, in my opinion, of much of the criticism you hear of it today. However, the colleges were crying for a single test which could be graded quickly and uniformly and which would closely correlate with academic success in college. These needs the aptitude test meets admirably.

"Actually, in judging a boy's academic ability, we give less weight to test scores than we do to his four-year high-school record. Besides, academic ability is only half of the matter; the other half is what we call promise as a person. You could sum up what we're after as brains *and* character. We don't put either one first. If high academic ability were the only criterion, we would have to eliminate quite a few future Presidents of the country and great college teachers, to say nothing of the boys of sterling personal quality Yale would be a poor place without. But high intelligence combined with imagination, vitality, a concern for others, and a capacity for growth—those are the things we're looking for.

"The more professional-minded you are as against what, at a loss for a better word, I'll call collegiate-minded, the more you'll weight the criteria for selection on the side of high academic achievement alone. This is, of course, the case with European universities—as it is with American graduate schools—where the student enters, with his general education completed, to pursue professional studies, living on his own in quarters of his own. The American college ideal, however, is living together and studying together a prolonged liberal arts and science program. Its concern is for educating the student as an individual, and its scheme is more humanistic and integrated in its operation."

Howe sighed. "Which would you take," he asked, "the lad with the high average and the good, sound personality who is going to do well as an undergraduate but never do very much afterward, or the boy who is a B-minus student in secondary school but may later catch fire intellectually—though perhaps not till graduate school—and never stop growing? Which would you admit, the millionaire's son who is rather supercilious now and is only mediocre academically but will one day fall heir to the means of doing great good for society, or the grade-hound? And what would you do about the honor-roll boy who has been 'motivated,' because his parents have been pushing him since infancy, and who has had good teaching, but whose aptitude tests suggest that his abilities are only mediocre? He's already reached his academic peak, so in his freshman year here he would be bound to level out and go down. He's what the guidance fellows call an 'over-achiever.' Those are a few of our problem boys. Sometimes I lie awake nights worrying about whether we've been kidding ourselves into taking a lot of brainy kids who are too egocentric ever to contribute much to society. Or have we been taking a lot of twirps who have read the how-to-get-into-college books, listened to their counselors, and learned to take tests and to give the right answers to interviewers—a bunch of conformists who will keep right on doing the smart thing for themselves? A prestige-college diploma is apparently considered the quickest way up the status ladder, and that's often what parents mean when they say they want their boys 'to have the opportunities that a Yale education offers.' This is perfectly understandable, but how far should a university go in accepting candidates whose reasons for applying are based on such shallow values? Should we admit them in the hope of changing those values, or do we get them too late to accomplish that?"

These unanswerable questions brought us to the more manageable ones of what sorts of backgrounds Yale applicants come from and how the admissions office seeks out the likeliest candidates. "A favorite word around here is 'diversity,'" Howe said. "First of all, we believe that our student body should be drawn from more than the five per cent of American families who can afford Yale. We know that a quarter of the country's highly talented youngsters never go to college, and one of our big jobs is to find some of these, interest them in Yale, and give them financial help if they need it. Sometimes we have to decide whether giving such aid is creating opportunity or causing injury. Take a boy, for instance, from a backward community or an uneducated family. Does he have the stamina to make the often painful adjustment to this highly articulate, sophisticated student body? And can he do it quickly enough to bring out his real distinction or will the academic and social competition here kill him before he gets off the ground? Those are some of the questions we have to ask ourselves. Geographical diversity doesn't mean too much, although our critics like to remind us that about half of our students come from the general area of the Northeast. But in the past we have enthusiastically grabbed what we thought was a North Carolina Tarheel, for example, only to discover that he was one of the thirty million Americans that had moved the previous year, and that he had been born and raised in Lynn, Massachusetts. What we're really after is diversity of talent and interest—boys with the unusual flair. They may be found in our back yard as well as in Sitka, Alaska."

Diversity of school background is another controversial subject, Howe continued. Of the past year's freshmen, forty-five per cent went to public high schools, forty per cent to private boarding schools, and fifteen per cent to private day schools or parochial schools. This, of course, means that the various types of private school supplied over half of the class, although such schools represent only twelve per cent of the country's secondary-school enrollment. Part of the explanation of this is simply that the private preparatory schools, as the name implies, specialize in preparing boys for the first-rate colleges, and are highly respected, educationally, by those colleges. But even these schools, Howe said, are having a lot of trouble these days getting as many students as they would like into Yale, Harvard, and Princeton.

I asked if there were any danger of producing a class which turned out to be heavily overbalanced in one direction, in microbiology majors, for example, or in graphic arts students. He replied that fortunately an average diversity could be assumed each year in a class of one thousand. About the same number of redheads, or twins, or forestry majors appear annually.

CHAPTER
THREE

CONCERNING the subject of Yale's relationship with the various secondary schools, Howe told me he thought I would learn a lot by talking to some of his assistants who annually spend the better part of their time between October and February hopping around among the various schools, interviewing boys who have already applied for Yale and seeking out promising youngsters who have not, in an effort to induce them to apply. The assistants' itineraries cover a constantly varying array of the nation's twenty-eight thousand or so secondary schools, and their routes range from the sedate Eastern prep-school belt to what they call "the dog-sled trip," around high schools in the far Northwest.

Before I saw Howe's assistants, I had a chat about Ivy League recruiting with Norman Harrower, Jr. (Groton, '40, Harvard '44), a former Navy flyer and recent member of the Harvard College admissions staff. As director of Yale's Office of Counseling and Placement and former assistant director of its Office of Financial Aids, Harrower frequently attends the admissions committee meetings. H.Y.P. and other top colleges scour the country and spend hundreds of thousands of dollars each year, he told me, to find the students with the high academic talent and personal strength which Howe had been describing to me. "This boy isn't such a remarkable fellow, basically," Harrower said. "He's no paragon. He's just the bright boy who settles down early and makes up his mind that he wants to grow up to be a pretty good kind of person. But he's in short supply. None of the top colleges is satisfied that it's filling its freshman class with a full quota of these youngsters. The Ivy League institutions know they are getting most of the Eastern supply even though they spend less money recruiting here than in the rest of the country put together. But we are not finding the numbers we should elsewhere—perhaps the boys there are going to state universities, perhaps they don't go to college at all. The more you hunt the more you feel that America's cultural pattern is not conducive to early maturity and hard mental work. There are schools in the country, of course, which maintain high expectations both of personal and academic development from their students. But in far too many today, social maturity is the prize."

The first of Howe's circuit-riding emissaries I talked to was Arthur F. Tuttle (Westminster '11, Yale '15), formerly a founder and, for many years, the senior master at Millbrook School, one of whose main concerns is liaison with neighboring prep schools. When he had welcomed me to his office, three doors down the hall from Howe's, he told me something about a practice called grouping, whereby Yale, in the fall, divides the applicants from fifty or sixty private and public schools whose high standards of preparation and reporting it can rely upon into A, B, and C groups, and practically guarantees admittance to the A group, in the hope that these youngsters will withdraw their applications to the other colleges if Yale is their first choice. Equally, Yale urges them to withdraw their Yale application if they have an A grouping from another college which is their first choice. This scheme, which is also followed by Harvard and Princeton, is based partly on preliminary aptitude-test scores obtained in the next-to-last year of secondary school, but it also requires some acute evaluation of each boy's talents by Yale staff men working with the school's principal, headmaster, or guidance counselor. "Before we consult with the latter, we spend about twenty minutes with each of the candidates for Yale at the school," Tuttle said. "Sometimes we work right around the clock until midnight. At the Choate School, for instance, which has some forty applicants for Yale this fall, it took two of us a day and a half to complete our interviews and grouping. These groupings we do on the spot are only tentative. When we get back to the office and some of the overenthusiasms we may have developed have had time to wear off a bit, we meet with the rest of the staff in a rump session of the admissions committee to go over all the groupings that have been made. Inevitably some boys' ratings are moved up and some moved down. Then we write letters to the schools formalizing the procedure. It's up to them to tell the boys or not as they wish.

"One reason we tend to trust the prep schools is that usually they have relatively few boys, and a good headmaster knows each boy," Tuttle added. "On occasion, for instance, I've rated a boy as a sure thing only to have a headmaster tell me, 'He's fine in an interview, but, frankly, I have doubts about how well he'd do at a place as big as Yale. His aptitude scores are O.K., but he won't work unless someone is breathing down his neck.' Well, that *is* the sort of boy who'd probably have trouble at Yale. If there are temporary reasons for a bright boy not doing his best—a death in his family, say, or a transfer in schools—the headmaster will tell me about them. And on the other hand, once in a while I've rated a boy B only to have the headmaster say, 'That's the most dependable student in our whole class.' There we've run into the problem of motivation—that B boy may turn out to be Phi Beta Kappa. We've found that the Phi Beta Kappas aren't necessarily those boys who arrive with the 800 college board scores. Many boys with scores in the 600's and perhaps not as well prepared for entrance as others, but who *want* to do a good job, are on the Dean's List and often make Phi Beta Kappa.''

I asked Tuttle how well grouping served its purpose of reducing the traffic jam of duplicate college applications. He said, ''It helps considerably, but there are still some kids who won't tell even their guidance man what their first-choice college is, because they're afraid that each college has a quota for each secondary school, and that if they announce their choice, they might influence too many others to apply from the same school, and so reduce their own chances. The fact is that we have no quotas of this kind—or of any other kind, for that matter—and if a school that sent us four boys last year has ten good ones applying this year, we'll take the ten. Then, some of the most brilliant boys simply like to collect admissions. Not long ago, one such kid stormed into the admissions office down at Princeton and said to Bill Edwards, the fellow in charge, 'I've been accepted at Harvard, Yale, and twenty other colleges. I want to know why Princeton has refused me.' The only thing I can say for this incident is that it refutes another bit of schoolboy folklore, which is that a youngster who is rejected by one of the H.Y.P. group will automatically be rejected by the others—that we operate some sort of secret boycott system. Well, anyway, we can't *make* the boys confine their applications to Yale. We think they should retain their freedom of choice, and, along with about a hundred and fifty other colleges, we've signed what is called the Candidates' Reply Date Agreement, which gives applicants until a set date around the middle of May to reply to admission offers from any of the member colleges.''

Tuttle's account of grouping moved me to hunt up later a guidance officer in one of the top high schools of the country to ask him how the scheme works from his point of view. He was enthusiastic. "We usually have fifteen candidates for Yale," he told me. "Generally four to eight of them are given A grouping. One of them, let's say, is Phil, whose first choice is Yale and second choice a college I'll call Old Ivy. I tell Phil he's been grouped A by Yale and that it would be helpful, if he's certain he wants Yale most, to withdraw from Old Ivy. But I warn him that once he's made his decision he must stick to it. So Phil withdraws from Old Ivy. That moves up Bob, whose first choice is Old Ivy, from sixth to fifth place on the latter's list of our candidates. Until now he's had very little chance at Old Ivy unless some of our top candidates were eliminated. That's exactly what's happened. Now everybody's happy. Yale puts Phil in its sure column, Old Ivy gets a fine lad it would have missed, and our batting average at both colleges has gone up."

At the end of my talk with Tuttle, he had said he wanted me to meet a colleague whose preoccupations were almost diametrically opposed to his own. This man, whom we found in a nearby office, was Warren Troutman (Cleveland Heights High School '35, Yale High Orations '39) a former member of the economics department at Ohio State University. He had returned not long before from the dog-sled trip. He told me that his fellow admissions men were a little tired of hearing about the hazards he faced in his travels, so he was delighted to have a new auditor. A typical day on the trail, he said, might include visits to four high schools, followed by dinner with a Yale alumni group, and then by a P.-T.A. meeting, or else by a particularly harrowing event called a College Night. At such a session, he explained, seniors from the various high schools in an area are assembled to hear addresses by various college representatives, each of whom is then assigned a desk, where he sits and answers the repetitive questions of youngsters milling about in a bargain-basement sort of fever. The usual attitudes toward Yale (as toward Princeton and Harvard), Troutman went on, fluctuate between polite interest, tempered by fear of the College Board exams, and outright suspicion of the university as the supposedly exclusive preserve of "snobbish, rich prep-school boys whose fathers all work on Wall Street." There are even a few regions whose school administrators are openly hostile to Eastern college representatives. However, in the hundred and twenty-five or so schools that Troutman visits annually he always finds a few interested students, and by talking with the four or five most promising boys in each senior class he usually elicits a number of additional applications, many of them accompanied by scholarship requests.

The educational scene which Troutman encounters on his trips is a constantly changing one. He spoke of a small Western high school which had sent Yale its first and only candidate in 1950. This fall, when he visited it, he found it twice its former size, illuminated for night football games, and proudly offering four good candidates. In the interval oil had been found nearby. In another section, a modest country day school with no more than two candidates annually in the past had renovated itself under a new headmaster and now had a good chance of ending the year with six successful applicants to Yale.

As Troutman and I were talking, I saw in the corridor the young interviewer who had so adroitly extricated the boy from the coat rack in the anteroom. Troutman beckoned him in and introduced him to me. He was Richard Moll, an alumnus of DePauw and Duke Universities, and the only non-Yale man (as well as the only graduate of Broad Ripple High School, Indianapolis) on the admissions staff. Moll, who is working for a degree in divinity and hopes one day to be a university chaplain, described to me one of the most strenuous interviewing sessions that the staff undertakes in the course of the year. This occurs when a couple of the men spend two days at the Boys' Club of New York, on East Tenth Street, where they talk to a hundred and fifty public- and private-school candidates from New York who can't get up to New Haven. The boys' reasons for being unable to make the trip range from arduous private-school schedules to inability to pay the fare (mostly the latter), and the boys themselves range from Collegiate School seniors to Harlem Negroes and Puerto Ricans, and sometimes include a number of orthodox Jews, wearing their skullcaps, who want to be sure that they can get kosher food at Yale and will not have to take tests on Saturdays. "About three-quarters of the boys we talk to at this session are applying for aid," Moll said. "A lot of them are so terrified by the interview that at the time we can get no idea of what they're really like."

Approximately sixty per cent of Yale's applicants come to the university, rather than let the university go to them, and now, with the admissions-committee meetings a few weeks away, Moll and his colleagues were seeing a total of perhaps twenty-five candidates a day. Moll said that the categories of applicants who particularly interested him, and who were therefore usually directed to his office, were handicapped lads, oddballs, boys from minority groups, and Hoosiers. One noon recently, he went on, he had returned to his office to find it aglow with abstract oil paintings, which had been lined up along the walls and propped on the chairs. Waiting to see him were a father and his crippled artist son, and the boy explained to Moll that he got about by means of a specially designed car, which was small enough, he hoped, to be permitted on the campus walks. After a long conversation, which revealed that the boy had realistically contemplated the sort of life he would lead at Yale, Moll took the father, the son, and the canvases over to the School of Art and Architecture, where they were enthusiastically received by the director. "There's one big problem," Moll told me. "The lad needs a companion to help him in the morning and at night, and extra quarters are not easily come by now. So I don't know how the admissions committee is going to feel."

Another unusual candidate he had interviewed recently was a twelve-year-old boy who kept jumping back and forth over the railings of the campus walks as he approached Welch Hall. "An amazing little kid!" Moll said. "His guidance man called up first, to tell us that the boy had exhausted the facilities—and the faculty—of his high school and that no one there knew what to do with him. Neither did his parents, who brought him in here. He had an almost comical way of gazing up at the ceiling and then looking at you hard, and almost at once he announced that he had two questions to ask me. First, he wanted to know if the Benjamin Franklin papers were kept in the closed stacks of the Sterling Memorial Library, and, second, he wondered if he could use the science laboratories at night for private research projects. I said I would find out the answer to the first question, and in reply to the second I gave a nice little sermon about how college was also a time for growing and living, and how working on lonely night projects could be a way of hiding from boys who were doing things natural for their age but not for his. With his permission, I took him over to see Dr. Bryant Wedge, the psychiatrist-in-chief at our Division of Student Mental Hygiene, who later told me that there was no question of the kid's ability to do college work but that he might adjust better here after a postgraduate year at some private secondary school. There the matter now stands."

Moll's mention of the Mental Hygiene Division prompted me to ask whether the university's psychologists and psychiatrists played any regular role in the admissions procedure. He said that although university psychiatrists were customarily asked to check over any applicants who might have been receiving psychiatric treatment, the main service that the psychiatric- and psychological-research sections performed for the admissions office was providing information on methods of personal assessment and discussing those methods with the admissions men in the light of student successes and failures. "We maintain that we can ordinarily predict how four out of five people will perform, even if we can't tell which one of the five will be the maverick," he said. "On the whole, though, we're pretty good at telling which group a candidate will fall into—the ranking scholars, the failures, or the pass boys. So we can say to a father, for instance, 'Your son's record is the kind that places him in the group where four out of five boys will fail. Unless there's something exceptional about him that will make us believe he may be the one boy in the group who *won't* fail, we can't afford to gamble on him, nor can *he* afford to have us do so.' It's no kindness to let a student in we feel may fail. If he flunks out of Yale, he's in the soup." The day is past, I learned, when a boy could flunk out of H.Y.P. and walk into "an excellent little liberal-arts college." Now, as a matter of institutional pride, even these schools want none of him. "Getting back to the subject of predictions," Moll added, "just as we can't always predict the failures, we can't always predict the geniuses. We can tell what ability-level group is likely to produce a genius, but not which boy in it will have the stability or the itch, the unhappiness or the happiness, or whatever it takes to keep him sweating until he creates something great." At this point Miss Bonnardi came in to tell Moll that there was another candidate waiting to be interviewed, so I said goodbye.

From these conversations and others with the staff I learned that every man has his own method of interviewing applicants. But whatever it may be, each concentrates first on putting a boy at his ease, no matter if he is the sort of youngster who walks in announcing heartily, with what he hopes is *savoir faire,* "Quite a layout you have here!" or the kind who sits mute with shaking hands and perspiring face. Probably no staff man has gone further in composing a taut young applicant than Donald R. Williams (Groton '23, Yale '27). During a recent interview he spent almost an hour reading through two large notebooks telling about the projected performances of the candidate, a young puppeteer, and then watched the boy open a satchel he had also lugged along with him, extract from it several puppets, and put them through their paces. On another side of the picture, some of the all-state athletes or the valedictorians who are scholarship candidates come to New Haven, as they do to other institutions on their list, frankly expecting to be bid for. One staff man mentioned that interviewing the top students from the foremost prep schools or from such great high schools as New York City's Stuyvesant or Walnut Hills in Cincinnati, which require entrance examinations, is sometimes a humbling experience. "You find yourself trying to soothe intellectual supermen," he said. He recalled one lad to whom he had put some routine queries designed to draw out candidates. For several minutes the boy sat in rigid concentration, and then said, "I can't answer your questions. They are ambiguous. In fact, they are ridiculous."

Some interviewers prefer if possible to visit with a candidate along with his parents for part of the appointment. "With luck we occasionally stumble on something we would want very much to know," said Tuttle, who likes at least to meet parents. "The other day, for instance, a boy came in with his father and mother, both of them uneducated, simple people. That lad did everything he could to let me know how proud he was of them." Other staff members find that a parent's presence only detracts from the interview. One of them told of a youngster who had come in with his mother. "We had hardly sat down in my office when the mother zipped open her large handbag and with an exuberant, 'Wait till you see how talented my son is!' brought out, one by one, thirty-five local newspaper clippings about his scholastic and athletic achievements. The boy curled right up inside himself. It was as though he had been struck. Afterwards, even though I *made* his mother leave the room, I could hardly get a word out of him."

An occasional parent goes to even more extreme efforts in his aspirations for his son, as I learned from Moll. He had recently been trying to obtain some foreign books in short supply. The agency man handling the transaction in a nearby city had been unusually obliging. Finally word came that the books had arrived and Moll hastened to the agent's office. There the latter, after carefully closing his door, announced that he was sure Moll would agree with him that he had done him a large favor. "One good turn deserves another," he said. "My son has his heart set on Yale." Opening up his desk drawer he pulled out a dossier on his boy complete with photographs from babyhood on. "The pitiful thing is that the boy is a great kid," said Moll. "The whole incident, which will do him no good, will have to be brought out at the committee meeting. The parental strategy here gives a slight insight into the boy's home life and background."

Some of Yale's interviewing is accompanied by a discreet use of the red carpet, cut to about the same pattern as at most top colleges—a conducted tour of the campus, visits to classes or professors in a candidate's field of interest, chats with an athletic coach if one is indicated, meals in one of the residential colleges, and perhaps an overnight stay in a small dormitory Yale keeps for the purpose. In a recent year the two top-ranking juniors and seniors from a greater part of Connecticut's high schools were invited to Yale for a Saturday program consisting of addresses from several distinguished faculty members and a tour of the university's facilities in the morning, and lunch and a football game in the afternoon.

CHAPTER

FOUR

HOWE had suggested that I come back the following week when he and the other staff members would tell me about the actual applications and how they are rated. Upon my return, the first person that Howe turned me over to was a small, graying woman named Miss Nellie Elliot, who, he said, had been a pillar of strength for six admissions chairmen since she joined the staff, in 1918. After Howe had left us, I asked Miss Elliot how many applicants she had interviewed over the years. "Oh, thousands, I imagine," she said, "but now I see only an occasional one. Some of them are candidates for the around fifteen undergraduate transfer openings we have a year, but mostly they are foreign students. I've always been interested in the foreign students, and I hope we'll always take at least twenty-five of them a year, as we do now. After they arrive, they keep dropping in here for a while. One day they stop, and then I know they're all right."

Coming to the subject of how applications for Yale are made, I asked first of all if there was any truth to the old stories about boys' being entered for the university at birth. Miss Elliot laughed, and said she had heard of no recent instances of this, although thirty or forty years ago it was not uncommon for a boy's name to be sent in to Yale the day after he was born, and the name of one member of the present senior class had been received when he was four years old. She told me something about this student's family and his secondary-school training—information that I later discovered she was able to supply about almost any of the current Yale men and many former ones. "A boy can give us his name whenever he likes," she went on. "All it means is that when we send out the formal application blanks—which we don't do until the September before the new freshman class is chosen—he is sure of getting one. Of course, long before September—in fact, all through the summer—boys are dropping in here. Many families nowadays take their sons on a grand college tour during the summer vacation. Not many years ago, our office didn't even stay open in summer. Now three or four of us must be here, to take care of a continuous string of interviews. The interviewing goes on right up until March 1st, but the application blanks must be in by around the first of the year. There's a ten-dollar application fee, which, of course, doesn't cover our administrative costs, any more than our present tuition charge of fourteen hundred dollars [since increased]—it's gone up from three hundred since my early days here—covers our instruction costs. But there are always some parents who feel obliged to protest. One of them wrote on his ten-dollar check this year, 'Payable only if my son enters Yale.' "

Miss Elliot produced a blank set of application papers, which ran to ten pages, for me to look at. The first two pages had the usual dozens of spaces for vital statistics and for information on the applicant's family and his schooling, including his significant school activities, the honors and prizes he had won, his hobbies and interests, his probable major, and the details of summer or term employment. There was as well a place for a photograph, and then came a page that was left entirely blank, for "any additional information which you would like brought to the attention of the Committee on Admissions." Miss Elliot said that only about a fifth of the boys filled out this page, and that many of these devoted it to a paraphrase of what the Yale catalogue said about the importance of a liberal-arts education. I noted with approval that Yale does not require the five-hundred word autobiography, a pious but aggressive intrusion into a student's privacy which some high-school guidance and college admissions men insist accompany application credentials and include, according to one set of instructions, a "description of your ambitions, your outlook on life, your sense of purpose, your relations with your parents, and how they developed." I noted with equal approval that there was no request in the Yale material for results of the so-called vocational interest tests or inventories, which supposedly measure a youngster's proclivities, and which many schools give their students in combination with special aptitude tests, in an attempt to predict in what fields of endeavor they are most likely to succeed. "Boys change too much at this age for us to be interested in what are, at best, only the tentative findings of such tests," Miss Elliot said.

The next pages had to do with application for financial aid, which, Miss Elliot said, was being requested this year by roughly forty per cent of the applicants. Here the student must first fill out a budget estimate, which includes the basic college fee [since increased] of twenty-three hundred dollars (covering tuition, room, board, and various health, laboratory, and insurance fees); a suggested four hundred and fifty dollars for books, clothing, entertainment, laundry, and such; and a travel allowance, varying with the distance between Yale and the boy's home town. From the sum of all these expenses, the candidate and his parents are instructed to subtract the amount they believe they can pay, ordinarily including two hundred and fifty dollars that the student is expected to earn in the summer and to contribute. The difference represents the amount of scholarship help needed. Except for a few special endowed grants, Yale offers no complete gift scholarships. Each scholarship boy must take a university job, at which he will work up to ten hours a week, the pay being credited against his tuition. Freshmen usually wait on table, and upperclassmen hold what Yale calls bursary jobs; that is, employment related to their own scholastic interests—research for an instructor in their academic field, say, or hospital work if they are premedics.

"The scholarship thing is terribly complicated, and often almost heartrending," said Miss Elliot. "An organization called the College Scholarship Service sends out and evaluates, for us and other colleges, a special questionnaire designed to check each family's financial status. It also puts out a manual to help colleges compute how much parents can pay, figuring in such factors as mortgages, the number of younger children, the age of the father, how to treat a widow's assets, and what not. But unfairnesses seem to be built into the situation. For instance, take two boys with identical qualifications whose families live in identical houses and have identical incomes. One family has spent every extra penny each year on vacations, home improvements, and so on, and is asking for fourteen hundred dollars in aid. The other family has scrimped along without these niceties and, over the years, has saved enough to reduce the aid needed to eight hundred dollars a year. We can try to balance things out by giving the boy from the happy-go-lucky family a five-hundred-dollar gift scholarship, a four-hundred-dollar long-term loan, and a five-hundred-dollar job, and the boy from the sacrificing family a five-hundred-dollar gift scholarship and a three-hundred-dollar job, but the inequity is still there. Or take the family whose mother has decided to go to work to pay the boy's college expenses. Even though we include only half of her earnings in our figure for the family income, still if we give her son the same scholarship sum we grant to a boy from a family with the same income whose mother *hasn't* gone to work, we are penalizing the first family for having an up-and-coming mother and for being sacrificing enough to do without her full-time care.

"And people have very different ideas of need. It's not uncommon to find a widowed nurse, making thirty-four hundred dollars a year and with two boys to educate, saying that she will contribute eight hundred dollars a year to one son's college costs, while a father in his middle thirties, earning twenty-five thousand dollars, and with assets of around a hundred thousand dollars, may declare that he can put up no more than five hundred dollars. Yale has a special form letter for these down-to-their-last-yacht parents, which flatly says we do not consider their sons entitled to aid. Then too, you'll notice that we like scholarship applicants who have worked and saved on summer jobs. But there's even an unfairness in that. In some parts of the country it's impossible for a boy who's a little young to get a regular unskilled job."

After the scholarship section, there are several pages for teachers and principals or headmasters to fill out, and as I looked through them, I thought they must have brought goose-pimples to many a boy as he dutifully delivered them to the addressees. The principal is asked to rank the applicant according to both "promise as a person" and "promise as a student," on a numerical scale of from 1 to 9, ranging from "outstanding" to "not recommended," and, in addition, to rank him in comparison with other Yale candidates at his school. The principal is also requested to write his estimate of the applicant's "character, intellectual promise, and industry as shown in his total school record," and to rank his ability in English composition from "below average" to "outstanding." On still another form, a teacher is asked to comment on the candidate's "intellectual curiosity, industry, integrity, concern for others, influence on others," and to make additional remarks in which "mention of any evident weaknesses will be welcomed." "We place considerable emphasis on these teacher evaluations," Miss Elliot told me. "The teachers, after all, see the boys operate from day to day in the classrooms, and the opinions they send us are free of the pressures that guidance men and administrators sometimes feel about particular boys." There are also on the forms generous spaces for the boy's scholastic record, and questions designed to help Yale evaluate his school's academic standards. These ask for such details as the length and frequency of the class periods, the passing and honors marks, whether the boy's class rank is figured only in competition with college-bound students, and a description of the content of the honors' courses.

Trying to judge a school academically can be an enormous problem, Miss Elliot explained, because of wide variations in such things as grading standards, passing marks (anything from 50 to 75), and course credits (which some otherwise reputable schools give for study that Miss Elliot, with a sniff, categorized as "basketweaving"). "When we have a boy who lists a senior program of English, journalism, speech, personality problems, marriage and family, and chorus, with his principal praising him to the skies, Mr. Howe sometimes writes asking why so able a boy is being given such poor preparation," she said. "Last week, we got an indignant response from one school saying that if we'd been more alert, we would have noticed that the boy in question had been elected president of the Student Council, so of *course* a light schedule had been planned for him!

"You'd be surprised how elementary some schools' idea of

honors work is," Miss Elliot went on. "Even excellent ones which should know better give extra math credit, for instance, for keeping the books for the school paper, or extra history credit for visiting the United Nations. And of course, it's a great deal easier to get a ninety average when your passing mark is seventy than when it's sixty.

"We don't ask the schools for detailed description of advanced placement courses. Those are the courses of actual college work which more and more schools are offering their bright seniors. The College Board does our work for us in evaluating these courses. It gives the students taking them Advanced Placement Tests, three-hour essay examinations with exacting standards. The candidates who pass them properly receive credit for a year of college work in each subject."

At that moment Miss Bonnardi came in to say that Miss Elliot's next caller had arrived. He was, I learned, a high-school guidance man in a pickle come to see if Yale could give him assistance. "We're delighted to," said Miss Elliot. "His plight is a good example of the pressure these men are under. A board member of his school is bringing him before a hearing on his competence. Last year he refused to back the application of the son of the board member to Yale. The boy's now at another college where he is doing C minus work. We've gone to the trouble of digging his folder out of the vaults. Well, he *might* have survived here, but only if he'd kept his nose to the grindstone day in and day out with no time for living at all. We support the counselor completely. We would never have taken the boy, and the guidance man was quite correct in not recommending him to us."

The problem of figuring out aproximately what a boy's school average means in terms of his ability to do Yale work has been energetically tackled, Miss Elliot had told me, by Associate Professor Paul Burnham, director of the university's Office of Educational Research, and after I had said goodbye to her, I stopped in to see Burnham, a scholarly-looking, spectacled man in his forties. He told me that since 1927 Yale has been carefully comparing its freshmen's grades with their previous secondary-school records, and has thereby been able to determine with a close degree of accuracy how the scholastic standards of several hundred schools compare with Yale's. "Let's take a hypothetical boy from a mythical prep school I'll call St. Swithin's," said Burnham. "His application tells us his average for his junior year there and the first semester of his senior year. First of all, we check over his transcript and cross out courses that we consider boondoggling. Then we take the average of the grades in those that remain, and if they have not been figured on a scale whose passing grade is 60, we reduce them accordingly. On the basis of our running comparisons of St. Swithin's standards with Yale's, we have worked out what we call an adjustment figure, which tells us what the boy's school average should mean in terms of Yale marks—a process that often brings the average down from 95 to 79, say. There are, though, two secondary schools in the country whose grading we consider tougher than ours, and we add one point to their students' average."

The process of adjusting the various schools' grades to the Yale standard is, I learned, no simple task. There are at least forty different grading patterns Burnham's office has to contend with, not to mention each school's interpretation of its pattern. Not only do some institutions have passing grades of 75 and others of 50, but an E can mean in turn excellent, passing, or failing. There are systems running A, B, C, D, and E, and E, D, C, B, and A, as well as numerical schemes of from 1 to 5 and from 5 to 1. Certain schools give letter grades for examinations and numerical grades for term marks, and others reverse the procedure. Some use percentiles; an occasional one finds a pupil's work satisfactory or unsatisfactory according to his potential or to his classmates' achievements;

and a few rate students into fifths on a group scale. Missouri stands by E, S, M, and G; the French have a scale of from 1 to 20; one establishment settles for plain Good and Bad; and English applicants to Yale often present the results of their Cambridge University matriculating examinations, which are so esoteric Burnham's office is unable to process them. Most of these many patterns are further complicated by the use of plus or minus to the extent even, in one instance, of a 1 minus rating higher than 1 plus. All of this welter Burnham and the office's administrative supervisor, Mrs. Marie Murdoch, take philosophically, remembering that not so long ago what were then Yale's own four undergraduate schools were each using different grading systems. Certainly the high point of the office's occasional frustrations was reached recently when, after some time of trying to reconcile conflicting reports issuing from a secondary school about its grading pattern, a letter was written its principal asking for a point-blank explanation. Rather plaintively the answer came back. To tell the truth, the principal wrote, he was confused too. If there was anything Yale could do to help his school straighten itself out in this matter, he would appreciate it.

Although the S.G.A., or School Grade Adjusted, as Burnham's final figure is called, is entered on the candidate's application records, its main importance, as far as Burnham is concerned, lies in its use, along with an applicant's College Board examination grades, in computing a prediction figure for the candidate's freshman-year average.

A little alarmed at such Orwellian evidence of scholastic determinism, I asked how accurate the freshman prediction figures usually turn out to be. "They're not perfect, thank goodness," he said. "It would be depressing if they were, wouldn't it? And please don't go away believing that these figures are necessarily a decisive factor in whether a boy is admitted to Yale, because ordinarily they're not. But I must say, in defense of our methods, that in recent years the individual predictions have consistently come within four points of freshman averages for half the class and within six points for two-thirds of it." Properly impressed, I said that making computations this accurate for several thousand boys must involve a massive arithmetical effort. "Well, yes," Burnham admitted. "Last year, as a matter of fact, we had to use twenty-five people and seven IBM machines to get all the figures onto the lists before the admissions committee met."

I next inquired about the statement that each year's freshman class was "the brightest ever." In response, Burnham rooted around in a couple of filing cabinets for a few minutes and came up with evidence that, at least statistically, the assertion was correct. Four hundred and eighty-eight members of the present freshman class, he said, had been predicted to make freshman averages of eighty or higher, as against three hundred and four members of the class of 1953, who had entered college ten years earlier. And so far, he went on, the present freshman seemed to be proving the forecast reasonably correct. There was other evidence, he added, cited by the Dean's office in support of its phrase "the brightest ever." In recent years the cut-off mark for making the Dean's honor list has had to be raised several points (it now stands at 83) to finally include the top twenty-five per cent of the class, and the grade average for the freshmen as a whole has risen five points to 78.3.

After I left Burnham, I decided to pay a call on a professor who had recently joined the faculty after several years at a large middlewestern university which has to accept almost any student from its state with a high-school diploma. Its freshman attrition rate reaches above forty per cent. In contrast, Yale's total freshmen failures amount to four per cent, with the flunk-outs only 1.7 per cent. I wanted to learn

if the professor had noticed any differences in his undergraduate classes at the two institutions. He told me that he
decidedly had. Before arrival at New Haven, he had up-
graded the undergraduate courses he was to give, increasing
the content, markedly raising the level of conceptual sophis-
tication, and tightening his marking system. Later he had
been forced to do so even more drastically, he said, after his
students themselves had told him his tests were too easy and
his markings too liberal. "At large state institutions, the
distinctive students tend to be in science," he said. "They are
often allowed to specialize as undergraduates long before
they are really educated. As a result the faculty has to cope
with the kind of problem this represents—an extreme example, I'll admit, but not too rare a one." He handed me a
composition that a freshman in a science class at his former
university had been asked to write as a commentary on the
course. It read:

"One thing I would like to have is longer hr in discussion
period. Lot of time we discuss a chapter after we had our
lab wrk. That a great help. Why can we have discuss on
chapter than lab work what we discuss not befo than. In lab
some time we don't know we are looking for cause we did
have discuss or read a text. Course as whole is very interesting, If we understand what we are doing and read that is
the reason we need longer hr in disc. It will help a person lot
to understand life. Lab work is interesting to some time it
was hard but I did care. That is call college."

CHAPTER
FIVE

HOWE had told me he would give me an idea, sometime that day, of the way the application folders are sorted and graded before the admissions committee makes its decisions. Before I learned about that part of the procedure, however, I felt I would like to talk to someone on the Yale faculty, preferably an irregular, about the admissions office's treatment of minorities. So I made an appointment with Professor Paul Weiss who had recently, on the request of President Griswold, investigated the position of Negroes in the college. Mr. Weiss is a systematic philosopher of world-wide repute, whose classes, as the *Yale Undergraduate* puts it, have "flabbergasted, infuriated, and charmed students" since 1946 when he joined the faculty after serving at Harvard and Bryn Mawr. He was now enjoying a term sabbatical preparing for a new philosophy-of-art course he was to teach, by taking instruction in painting, dancing, sculpting, and acting. I found him, a short, darting man, wearing spectacles, in an old-fashioned office. "I'm interested in all minorities, not just Negroes," Weiss told me without preamble. "There's an anecdote about Levi Jackson, Yale's first Negro football captain and a New Haven boy, which I think will tell you all you need to know about Yale's attitude toward colored students. New Haven's Negroes were naturally very proud of Levi Jackson. So they took up a collection to buy him a Cadillac. Jackson explained to them that he couldn't accept such a gift and suggested instead that they establish a scholarship with the money. 'Great! A Yale scholarship for a New Haven Negro boy,' they replied. 'Now see here,' said Jackson, 'when you limit your scholarship to a Negro you are guilty of race prejudice. Why don't you make it a scholarship for *any* needy New Haven boy?' So they did. Yale is democratic," continued Weiss. "There are no rooms kept here just for scholarship boys. You can make a secret society even if your father is a cab driver—not that I approve of secret societies. I've never found any prejudice in the admissions office. They know over there that a good college needs irregulars. People ask me to look into cases of boys from minority groups they think may have met with prejudice in admissions. I go right over to the office and we get out the boys' folders and examine them together. I've always found just reasons why the students were rejected.

"But I have one criticism about the office. It's honeycombed with Yale graduates, and they know little about how underprivileged people live and think. When I was a poor boy on the lower East Side in New York City—my father was a laborer—I would never have dreamed that Yale would want me as a student. Now I think—or rather hope—that if I were that same boy today Yale *would* want me. But what does the bright Southern Negro boy or the poor white youngster in the cotton fields know about Yale? We need new, imaginative methods to find these boys and bring them here. Yale would be good for them—it's good at integrating, synthesizing, civilizing."

Since I knew that Weiss lived at one of the residential colleges, before I left him I asked how he found the undergraduates today. Outside of wishing that there were more foreign students among them and more boys who wanted to spend their lives as scholars, he said he found them admirable. "They are keen, intelligent, and most of them want to be well-rounded and successful. You'll find the intellectuals here over at the gym doing body-building exercises or swimming in their spare time. Even the athletes take some hard courses—they'd be ashamed not to. Everybody listens to music all the time, by the way. Whoever said they were the 'silent generation'? My classes pop with their questions. They want to discuss all the basic problems—what is God, what is morality. But no one knows his Bible any more—that surprises me—and no one knows how to spell. No one today even knows how to spell 'existence'."

When I found Howe back in his office, he lost no time in settling me down to learning about the intricacies of grading the application folders before the final committee meetings. "By now, we have almost all the information we're going to get on the boys, except for the results of their College Board achievement tests in high-school subjects, and those scores will soon be coming in," he told me. "We have the school records, résumés of interviews, aptitude-test scores, and preliminary predictions by Burnham's office. There are also reports on candidates from alumni groups, whose role in all this Waldo Johnston, the director of our University Committee on Enrollment and Scholarships, will tell you about shortly. Well, from now right up until the admissions committee meets, members of our staff, along with the six faculty and administration members who are on the admissions committee but are not on our staff, will be reading and rating the folders. Ordinarily, each folder is read by at least two people, and each reader writes on a big work card his general impression of the boy concerned, along with an A, B; or C rating for admission, and, if the folder includes an application for a scholarship, the amount of aid he believes we should give. On the same card, the boy is also given a numerical rating on his general promise as an individual, estimated on the basis of interviews, the reports of those who know him, and whatever else we have gleaned about him. Incidentally, if two folder readers disagree on whether a boy should be rated A, B, or C for admission, or if they are more than a hundred dollars apart on the scholarship figure, Johnston or I read the folder and adjudicate. We estimate that about a fourth of the nearly five thousand boys applying this year will be rated A, and that almost half, who are obviously in the lower half of the competition (though still frequently good candidates) will be rated C and rejected. Now, we assume that three or four hundred of the A boys will decide to go to other colleges, so this means that around that number of B candidates can be added. This sorting out of the Bs is our toughest job."

The decisions about which of the Bs make the grade, Howe said, depend not only on their personalities and their scholastic credentials but on the geographical and educational diversity of their backgrounds, which he had discussed earlier; on the need for strengthening existing links with schools or alumni groups, or establishing new ones; and, in a good number of cases, on whether the applicant's father happens to be a Yale alumnus. Yale announces in its admissions booklet that preference will be given to alumni sons "who meet admissions standards," and although, as Howe explained, the college is now tougher than ever before in judging these "legacies," and admits proportionately fewer of them, they still make up about twenty per cent of each freshman class, as they also do at Harvard and Princeton.

Howe now directed me to the office of Waldo Johnston, the man principally responsible for liaison with the alumni.

Johnston, who was wearing a Yale blazer that bore the crest of Davenport College, told me that he had come to his present job from the post of executive secretary of the Alumni Board, and that before joining the Yale staff he had been assistant headmaster of the Pomfret School. The University Committee on Enrollment and Scholarships, which was started by Yale in 1943 as a pioneering venture and has since been copied by other prestige colleges, consists of eleven hundred alumni, in all parts of the country, who interview about three thousand candidates every year. "They often find promising lads we wouldn't have found on our own," Johnston said. "And even more often they give us realistic, first-hand appraisals of boys we don't know enough about, or boys who are being too highly touted by their schools. In fact, the committee was started after we found ourselves admitting too many boys who were well qualified from the academic point of view but not from any other. Of course, we do want outstanding scholars, but how are we to find out more about the *spirit* of a candidate—the selflessness, integrity, and honesty that are so badly needed in this day of false ideals? It's in making this sort of judgment of candidates that the alumni interviewers fill an important need. We realize that such judgments are very hard to make, and naturally the alumni vary sharply in their skill at making them. But we come to know each interviewer's prejudices and predilections pretty well, and are able to make allowances for them."

In addition to their annual gifts to Yale, which in recent years have totaled over two million dollars a year, the alumni make available to each freshman class scholarships amounting to around fifty thousand dollars. I asked Johnston how the recipients of these grants were selected. He said the procedure was the same as for other candidates, bearing in mind that scholarship recipients were expected to have even higher academic and personal promise than applicants not requesting aid. "Each year the local alumni committees who have scholarships available send us a list of the boys they consider likely candidates for them. We try to let the committees know as early as possible how their candidates seem to us. If they look mediocre or if they have no chance at all, we tell the alumni so. Sometimes that only stings them into frantic action. They marshal their forces and get everyone they can think of to write in letters praising their boys. Well, there's an old saying that the thicker the folder, the thicker the candidate." Only rarely any more, Johnston continued, does a local committee balk at giving its scholarship money to a boy the admissions office has approved for aid. Should such an impasse arrive, the alumni group may withhold its award for that year, but the candidate to whom it has refused aid will be found some other grant by the office.

The two most frequent sources of friction between the admissions office and the alumni are legacies and athletes. "The rejection of one legacy whom the alumni in his area consider well qualified can do more harm than we can offset by letting in ten local non-alumni sons," Johnston said. "Consequently, we often take ten times as long in deciding to reject one Yale son as we do in deciding to admit someone else. At the end of our two-week admissions-committee meetings, we spend at least half a day reviewing the legacies we've turned down." Last year, he told me, Yale admitted over two-thirds of the four hundred and twenty-eight alumni sons who applied—a ratio that is closely paralleled at Harvard and Princeton. I told him I'd recently heard that at Princeton a disproportionately large number of alumni sons flunked out or were placed on probation, and he answered that although the situation was not too different at Yale, there were still a sizable number of legacies in the top quarter of each class.

As for athletes, Johnston continued, when an influential

alumnus in his forties or fifties writes in enthusiastically about what he calls "a well-rounded boy," the chances are very strong that the boy in question is a football player. "Those alumni were undergraduates in the days of T. A. D. Jones, Albie Booth, or Clint Frank, when football was a religion here and the Bowl its shrine," he said. "By now, we've patiently pointed out to almost all of them that we're perfectly happy to have them find us athletes as long as the athletes can make satisfactory showings on their College Boards and will study as hard as everybody else after they're admitted. The odds are against our admitting anyone whose College Board average falls below 550, though we have no rigid cutoff point. Anyway, we certainly don't dislike athletes. Eighty per cent of the undergraduates here engage in athletics of some kind, many as members of the residential college teams in fifteen different sports. In a group of similarly qualified candidates, an outstanding athlete—or, for that matter, an outstanding clarinettist—will probably be the one we choose, because we believe that unusual achievement in any field shows unusual self-discipline and suggests a contribution to and benefit from activities which the college respects."

For years, Johnston said, Yale has had a rule that no athletic coach can institute recruiting, but if a young athlete has written to a coach, or has formally applied for admission, the coach is free to correspond with him—to send him monthly department letters and game programs, keep him aware of the admissions-committee deadlines he must meet, and urge on him the virtues of Yale. This gentlemanly assault is conducted by mail, and the inducements that the university offers are strictly limited to hard work on the playing fields and hard work in the arts and sciences the rest of the time. Since this Spartan routine has been known to appear less than enticing in comparison with such goodies as special scholar-

ships, special jobs, specially paid trips to the campus, and
special blocks of seats at athletic events, all of which are
lavishly dispensed by some universities, I decided to ask Yale's
athletic director, DeLaney Kiphuth, how he believed his department was faring under the enforced separation of admissions and athletics.

Kiphuth who is also a lecturer in history, and is the son
of Yale's famous swimming coach Robert Kiphuth, met me
in his office in a small building near the Payne Whitney
Gymnasium. When I had told him what I wanted to know,
he handed me a copy of the regulations of the eight-member
Ivy Group, which since 1954 has forsworn both athletic
scholarships and extra-remunerative jobs for athletes. Among
other things, the regulations stipulate that each varsity athlete has to file an annual statement listing all sources, other
than his parents, of gifts, loans, or other contributions toward
his expenses, as well as a complete list of these expenses.
"Of course, we hope we never have an admissions committee
made up of the sort of people who drop dead at the sight of
an athlete," Kiphuth said. "We let Arthur Howe know early
in the year about boys we'd particularly like to see at Yale,
and ask him to tell us if any of them look too weak scholastically, so we can suggest that they apply elsewhere. Then,
just before the committee meets, I send over a list of the
boys each coach is interested in, and when the meetings are
over, Arthur tells us who's been admitted. We have a lot of
disappointments every year. But every year, too, boys turn
down scholarships elsewhere to come here, because they want
no part of the curfews, the segregation into athletic dorms,
the supervision of academic programs, and the general feeling of being paid hands that an intelligent human being who
is also a good tackle or halfback might get at one of the big
football factories.

"The Yale athlete comes right out of the normal educational

community," Kiphuth continued. "No one looks up to him as a hero, and he doesn't even wear a sweater with a letter around the campus. There's no physical education major here for him to take refuge in as there is at some institutions," he said, handing me a record of an athlete at a large state university who had written in with the thought of transferring to Yale. In the first semester of his freshman year I saw that he had taken Remedial Rhetoric and Composition, Personal and Community Hygiene, Swimming, Physical Conditioning, Freshman Drill and Theory, and a course called Professional Orientation. His second semester had included Greek and Roman Sports, Camp Counseling, Public Health, Beginning Football, Beginning Basketball, and Principles of Effective Speaking. He was enrolled in Indoor and Outdoor Recreational Sports and Principles of Recreation during his sophomore year; was repeating Remedial Rhetoric and Composition; and apparently was conditioned in Anti-Aircraft Artillery, and History of the United States.

"A coach can't be happy here unless he is the kind of man who doesn't want to own a lad, which is about what it amounts to when a college admits a boy to play a sport," Kiphuth said. "I have a lot of sympathy and respect for the fellow running a 'big time' program with a clearly defined group of boys imported to staff the teams. It's a hard and demanding job that requires a lot of ability. I don't think, however, that it belongs in an academic institution and I'm glad we don't have it. I enjoy seeing what the regularly enrolled boy can do when he tries his hand at athletics and what lessons he will learn therefrom to carry into his career in law, medicine, business or teaching. Incidentally, the demands put on a coach by all these bright athletes with their exacting academic schedules are terrific. For one thing, a coach has to be a lot better teacher than he used to be. And he must be a very resourceful man on the practice field. He has to organize the time there so that every minute means something. In football, for instance, training has been condensed to one and a half hours on the three heavy practice days a week, and to less on the other days. And of course, the Ivy League has long since done away with spring practice and post-season bowl games."

Kiphuth took me down the hall to meet James G. Holgate, the head freshman football coach, on whose desk lay a large book of newspaper clippings and a pile of sports pages. I found that he had just been looking at a film of a Southern high-school all-star game which a coach had sent him. "Naturally, we try to keep track of promising players," he told me after Kiphuth had gone back to his own office. "And this applies even to prep schools, which are frankly a bone of contention between us and the admissions department. We aren't allowed to have any contact with prep-school boys. That's because Arthur Howe feels that his office is in very close touch with the schools anyway and that any such contact might give the boys misleading ideas about the role of athletics in admissions."

Holgate went on to tell me about the encounters an Ivy League coach is apt to have with candidates today. "Lots of times a boy we're excited about may arrive in New Haven for his interview and then come over here to see us. But before we have a chance to show him the gym, the swimming pool or the stadium, he may ask to see the chemistry labs. It turns out he's going to be a metallurgy major, say—which may mean he'll be doing some twelve hours of laboratory work a week. Just that announcement, by the way, would have cured his chances with the big football factories. 'Drop the chem and the metallurgy,' they would have told him, 'or there will be no scholarship from us.' Well, the boy may enter Yale all right. But *we* may never see him again. He may decide that the fishing team or the parachute jumping club offer him the greatest challenge," said Holgate resignedly. "But then again he may come out for football in spite of the metallurgy major and a ten-hour bursary job to boot. He may have to study until 1:30 at nights, but most important, he'll have to learn how to schedule his time effectively. Achieving the latter is the key factor in first-year college adjustment. The encouraging fact is that thousands of Yale students have been and will be successful in proving that taking a tough course with labs, carrying a work job, and still playing an intercollegiate sport *can* be done."

Holgate went on to say that a tremendous amount of mail concerning football players is constantly coming in from all over the country. More and more boys are going out for the sport, every year, particularly in public high schools. He showed me several examples of the mail. One, a mimeographed letter from a coach, with a boy's photograph pasted on it, gave detailed statistics about its subject's running, passing, and punting records. "This same coach put out a newspaper story a few weeks ago saying that the kid already had sixty schools after him," Holgate said. "It's his way of advertising both the boy and himself. Some parents, too, are very businesslike in the way they shop around for colleges. I'm sure a father wrote this one." He handed me a sheet labeled "CONFIDENTIAL!" and I read its final paragraph: "This lad has a 92 average, varsity letters in football, basketball, and baseball, and is excellent material for your consideration. They want him at Holy Cross, Colgate, Michigan State, and Boston College, but he would go great at Yale." A piece of lined notebook paper he next handed me was a communication from a boy himself. "Dear Coach," it read, "I am ready to start making touchdowns for dear old Yale if you can give me a scholarship. I am a good kicker and speedy half back. I would like to come and meet you coaches and visit the campus. If you can take care of my expenses I will be Yale's next All American."

"This is the kind we are more apt to pay serious attention to," Holgate said, passing me a handwritten letter from a coach in the Far West, about a boy I'll call Rodney Carlson, which read, "Rod is a student leader and a typical young American of whom we are proud. He has a respectable average of 92 plus, and has been our center for three years. He has performed tremendously, being the best lineman in our history. He has speed, drive, and hitting force, and is the team's fireman."

"Our alumni representative out there is very impressed with Carlson," Holgate told me, "and we've had several letters from the boy himself. He's quite interested in Yale, and I hope we get him."

I thanked Holgate, and made a mental note to try to read Carlson's folder and keep track of how he fared through the admissions process.

CHAPTER
SIX

WHEN I returned to New Haven in late March for my stint of folder reading, the door of the admissions office bore a notice to the effect that no more candidates would be interviewed. Inside, except for an occasional headmaster or guidance man who arrived, sometimes with a youngster in tow, for a last-minute review of his school's grouping in the light of new exploits or disappointments among his candidates, I found only members of the admissions staff and a few other people, who, I later learned, were members of the admissions committee. The composition of the committee varies annually, but it always reflects as many as possible of the interests and pressures bearing on selection. Usually it consists of two or three men from the admissions office and five or six from other divisions of the university's administrative and academic staff, including three faculty members (two of them from the engineering and scientific departments), serving three-year terms; representatives from both the Freshman Dean's office and that of the Dean of Yale College; and a master of a residential college, a faculty member who can bring to the board's deliberations the additional viewpoint of students' everyday lives with their peers. Most of the committee members I saw were deeply involved in the same task I had come for. Miss Bonnardi welcomed me, led me into a room lined with filing cabinets, which contained the folders of the applicants, and introduced me to Mrs. Marjorie Heywood, a calm, white-haired woman, who has charge of the files. Mrs. Heywood settled me at an empty desk and brought me a couple of armloads of folders that she had picked out at random, along with Rodney Carlson's folder, which I had asked to see.

As I studied the seven or eight documents in each folder, I was continually astonished at how sharply the personalities of the boys whose photographs stared out at me were conveyed by their answers to the form questions and by the comments of their various teachers and interviewers. In laboriously careful handwriting, the applicants announced that their hobbies were whistling in the shower, hunting, fishing, foreign cars, progressive jazz, reading; that they had had summer jobs in motels, in lumberyards, on construction gangs; and that they wanted to be financial experts, engineers, diplomats, teachers, doctors, lawyers, businessmen. Outside of the few who were clearly overreaching themselves, and whose work cards I was not surprised to find marked C and bearing some such comment as "Except for the fact his father is Yale '33, there's not much here," or "Too bad. A perfectly nice lad, but that's about the extent of it," I would have admitted them all. From the folders marked A, I usually got an impression of solidity, purpose, and talent, together with a bursting vigor or a questing thoughtfulness. These qualities managed to emerge through even such assembly-line jargon of guidance men as "Very interested in subject matter and in content and is most effectively motivated toward those goals. Strong leadership potential." There was, for instance, a big blond boy with classical features who was a crack football guard and of whom his teacher said, "He shows unusual intuition in translating the most subtle lines of contemporary French poetry. He is strong physically and emotionally and has a perfect inner balance. He's full of refreshing naturalness, quietness, and goodness." Then, there was a freckle-faced three-letter man who "has a brilliant mind and imagination and is the most original thinker in his class," according to *his* teacher's report, which continued, "His fine brain is not entirely in focus. When it becomes so, he will function at the very top academically." Both of these boys had College Board aptitude-test averages of over 700, and both were ranked one for promise as students and as persons by their schools. One had a 94 school average, the other a 92—though I noticed that Burnham's predictions had tumbled their probable Yale averages to 85 and 80.

Besides ranking the folders an over-all A, B, and C for admission and scholarship, the readers mark the candidates on a scale of from one to nine for "personal promise." The Yale rating is also tighter on this score, I found, than is that of most secondary schools. Both of these lads, for instance, had got only a two from their readers. I never, indeed, found a one ranking even on the A folders I read carrying such enthusiastic comments as "The kind we want—bright, interesting, personable and self-reliant," or "A quiet, thoughtful boy who would prosper here and be a very fine influence. Topnotch prospect."

From some of the C folders came a youthful sense of failure. A boy in the middle of his class at one of the country's top schools wrote that although he realized he was not a "prime candidate," he was now working hard, and promised to do all within his power, "God willing, to bring honor to myself and to Yale." Another C boy had been marked 4 as a student and 7 as a person by his school guidance man, who finished him off with the dismal summary "This boy reflects sincere motivation in verbal areas, but not in others." This meant,

I realized as I read further in the folder, that the boy wanted to be a writer, and found mathematics and science dull fare. The grade that Burnham had predicted for him was 75—just under the Yale freshman-class average of 78.3. The first folder reader had rated him B, but the second, who had apparently interviewed him, had rated him C, calling him "a sloppy, unprepossessing lad, very talkative and only sometimes interesting." Howe had adjudicated the case, reluctantly confirming the C rating. "I suppose the school is right in saying there's too much dreaming and too little real work," he noted. "But the boy is different enough to add something to Yale, and his father, a writer, says right now his son is a better writer than he is. He would be an academic risk, but an interesting gamble." To one C folder, an alumnus who was not a member of the Committee on Enrollment and Scholarships had contributed a gung-ho epistle that began, "I like the cut of this boy's jib! His father is a father of men!" The regular alumni interviewer had evidently looked a little deeper into both the father of men and his offspring. His report said, "This is an attractive chap in spite of his father, who is a bit too smooth. But there are certain things about him which make me believe that he will shy away from any subject when the course becomes difficult, and also influence others to take the easy way out. He was, for instance, offered the advanced-math course but declined it, even though he wants to do graduate work in science, because he said he could not afford to risk getting a low mark." Still another lad rated C, who wrote on his application form that he "was not one of the boys," was described by his alumni interviewer, through various circled adjectives in a series on a printed form, as "sensitive," "frail," "intellectual," "odd," "eccentric," and "neat." The man had written, "Surely there is room for a boy like this in a university as large as Yale.

I expect him to make no contribution as an undergraduate, but he will be heard from in later life."

Occasionally evidence turned up in the folders of alumni interviewers having struggled against a personal distaste for a candidate. From a western state where the interviewing is done by a committee of alumni, the chairman highly recommended the outstanding student in the local school of 2000 "even though three of us took an active dislike to him and found him very disagreeable."

I found a number of ratings that rather surprised me, and I was particularly perplexed by two. The first was that of a boy I shall call Ned Summers, from a large, excellent Middle Western high school, who had maintained high honor marks since the ninth grade, and had a 95 school average and a prediction of 87 as a Yale freshman. In his College Board aptitude tests, he had scored 796 in verbal ability and 750 in math. His school rated him 1 as a student and 4 as a person, and described him as having an "unusually keen, analytical, and logical mind," average maturity, and an influence on his peers "less than his ability warrants." Also, he evidently had some artistic talent. A teacher commented, "Ned is still awkward and inarticulate, and occasionally earns the disdain levelled at him by his classmates, since he does not always gracefully accept deserved criticism. But for the most part he is friendly, socially acceptable, pleasant, and intent on doing a good job. It's hard to be a bright boy!" In spite of all this, the Yale interviewer would have none of him. "I would prefer to see this lad go to Harvard," he wrote. "He's inarticulate and uninteresting—a grade-grubber." Ned had originally been rated B, but the second reader had given him only C.

The second case that perplexed me was none other than that of Rodney Carlson, the football player. His photograph showed him to be a big, solemn-looking lad, and his record was, at first glance, overwhelming. His high-school average was 93, and he stood thirty-fourth in a class of over five hundred. "My first impression was that this boy would make an excellent tackle for any Big Ten team but that he might be over his head at Yale," the office interviewer had written. "This notion vanished almost as soon as he opened his mouth. He is an extremely bright young man. He is an accomplished cellist and has written compositions for both this instrument and the tuba, which he's performed with a college orchestra. A nice lad, clean-cut and a solid citizen." An alumni interviewer described Carlson as a "quiet, reserved, humorous, friendly lad who does not enjoy talking about himself," and added, "I am obviously rather impressed with him." He ended his eulogy with what seemed to be an understatement: "He has, I feel, exceeded the level of individual output for most high-school students." The list of Carlson's junior and senior activities took up more than seventeen typed lines. He not only had found time for football, basketball, and track but had also managed to serve as prom king, president of the Latin Club, president of the junior class, president of the Student Council, president of the school orchestra, vice-president of the school honor society, class historian, chairman of the assembly committee, president of a church youth organization, president of the drive for American Field Service exchange students, and so on and on. Carlson, who was applying for aid, had been rated no better than B, with a scholarship of fourteen hundred and fifty dollars recommended. Arthur Howe had written on his work card, "This is about the biggest B.M.O.C. I ever saw." (The initials, I eventually realized, stood for "Big Man on Campus.") The second reader asked, "Can he stay in college?" I then looked up Carlson's College Board aptitude scores, and found that they were only 487 for the verbal test and 562 for the math.

At that point, Howe came into the room, carrying a well-stuffed briefcase and looking harassed. After a glance at the pile of folders I had read, he commented jokingly on how little headway I seemed to have made. "We break in our new people by having them read folders for several solid months," he said. "After they've been with us about three years, they get so they can average ten or fifteen an hour. This year, I've given instructions that we must be unusually tough in our ratings, because the competition is stiffer than ever. I'm worried to death for fear we'll be stuck with too many A candidates. It's going to be murder to cut them down. We spend two days before the meeting roughly totalling up what we have. Then the committee always knocks down a few boys and moves up considerably more. And of course, that means even *more* cutting back at the very end." He added that no one on the staff could spare the time just then to answer any questions I might have, but that he would arrange for Ernest F. Thompson, an Associate Freshman Dean who had formerly served on the admissions committee, to drop by and see me that afternoon. Thompson, who, I learned, is a New Zealander, and a member of the Yale faculty of sixteen years' standing as a lecturer in zoology, oceanography, and meteorology, turned out to be a tall, ambling man, dressed in tweeds and a plaid shirt, with sandy hair falling over his forehead and a face that looked as though it had been carved by sea spray. When I told him of my perplexity over some of the ratings, he was amused and sympathetic. "Even after years of experience," he said, "you sometimes have the nasty feeling that you could take all the thousands of work cards—except those for the five hundred students at the top of the list and the five hundred at the bottom, whose ratings nobody could honestly question—and you could throw them down the stairs, pick up any thousand, and produce as good a class as the one that will come out of the committee meeting." He asked which folders were troubling me, and I handed him the

Carlson lad's dossier. After scanning it, he left to get the boy's freshman prediction figure, which had not yet been entered in the folder, from a file in another room. "His prediction is 61," Thompson said when he returned. "Under the circumstances, I'm afraid he won't make it. Everybody liked him, it's true, and it might be a case where you could say we're being too stuffy about academic requirements. But if you consider it a bit, there's something monstrous about all that activity. And how did he ever get that 93 average, anyway? In fact, how did the boy ever have time to read a book?"

Next, I handed Thompson the folder of Ned Summers, the awkward, inarticulate youth with the 87 prediction and 796 English score whose alumni interviewer hoped he would go to Harvard and who had been lowered to a C rating. "I suspect that the committee is going to have quite a discussion about this lad," Thompson said. "Sometimes you can't give any logical reason for feeling uneasy about a boy, and making a decision against him. But, you see, your mind stores up the histories of fellows you've known here. Somewhere there is a mental picture of a boy like this who clearly would have been better off, as Yale would have been, if he'd gone to another college."

Thompson laid the folders aside for a moment. "From the vantage point of a faculty member," he said, "the admissions situation seems so simple. Just reject the bottom third of the class and the bad characters, and there you are. Well, it doesn't take much experience of working with the committee to realize that it's impossible to predict always just which boys, once they are admitted, will fall into that bottom third of the class which the faculty thinks we could do without. There are certain groups of boys we're apt from experience to be cautious about, but we certainly can't exclude all the boys in them because we know that sometimes these groups produce failures, or, more often, account for a good deal of the bottom third of the class. As you've probably heard by now, the boy with the modest test scores and the consistently high secondary-school grades may be a gamble because he may already have stretched as far intellectually as he can. The badly prepared boy with the high scores presents another kind of problem. He must make up his deficiencies before he has a chance of reaching his true potential. But just how far is a university committed to offer freshman make-up courses for such a student, and what is it missing if it doesn't offer them? Another boy we worry about is the middle-stand student with the high college boards, who has been spreading himself thin in secondary school in many extracurricular activities. At best the latter are only a pale image of the entice-ments the Yale community will lay before him. Will he chan-nel his energy into academic work here or will he go bursting off in any number of directions with barely a toehold in the bottom of the class?"

He went on to tell about an instance at a committee meet-ing some years ago that illustrated the imponderables in the selection process. A borderline boy was up for decision. He was president of his class and his prediction for Yale was 70. Though his aptitude scores were high, his achievement-test marks were low, and his school average was a bare C plus. One of his teachers insisted that when the boy found his field he would make unusual contributions, and there was appar-ently something manly and distinctive about him that had won over both his alumni and staff interviewers. At the height of the discussion over him, a new faculty member of the committee broke into impassioned speech. It was irrespon-sible even to consider admitting such a gamble, he exclaimed. Yale should be accepting only the cream, boys like a present senior and major in his department whom I will call **Dan Morton**, who had done distinguished service in the Yale community and had just received a coveted award for graduate study abroad. The professor stopped in amazement when more seasoned members of the committee began to laugh. "Morton had been practically the borderline boy's duplicate," Thompson explained. "His prediction figure had been only 62. But we took a flyer on him and it paid." I asked if the committee had voted to give the other boy the same break. He had been rejected, Thompson said. In the years between the two cases the tide of quality had crept up.

Howe had told me earlier about the pleasure he took in spotting these able late bloomers, so-called, and in doing what he could to help them along the road to maturity. "Particularly the ones," he said, "who don't deserve admission to Yale when they apply, but who we think in the long run are going to turn out to be much better persons than many boys we take who've done all the right things. I like to send these young-sters out to pasture for a couple of years to grow up—to join the armed services, dig a ditch, work in a factory, or maybe travel—and then see them enter here and perform way up to their potential. We think we catch some considerable talents in this way we would otherwise miss. Two years ago we had such a boy, the son of a Pittsburgh family of well-known Yale benefactors. There was good stuff in him, but there had always been too much money, too much pressure, and too much expectancy that he would add to the family's accom-plishments. So he was all fouled up. Though his college boards were all right, his school record was terrible. Almost everything was wrong. He had flunked out of his first prep school and hardly done a lick of work through his second, where he stood last man in his class. We told his family we saw no reason to expect that a thirteenth year of formal edu-cation just then would do what the past twelve had failed to do, and urged him instead to join the army. He did. When he had finished his two years, we saw him again and suggested he bone up for several months at a tutoring school. If that turned out all right, we told him we would consider him. Just before college opened, we admitted him. When his Yale counselor's first-year report on him came in, we particularly liked the opening sentence: 'You can imagine my shock when I first opened his folder and saw his prediction was 57!' The counselor then went on to speak of the boy's maturity, his conscientiousness, and his hard, creative work, and added, 'His average is 82.' And that's where it's stayed ever since," said Howe with satisfaction.

Returning to the folders, I asked Thompson about one of a B-rated prep-school boy whose father, I knew, was also one of Yale's important benefactors. The boy himself wrote, in his application, "All my life I have had things too easy. My parents tended to spoil me, treating me more as their friend than their child and making little effort to develop in me the self-discipline that would have helped me form study habits. Now I have to do the job myself. I began it last year. It's a slow task, but I am sure I will complete it." The staff man who had visited the applicant's school wrote of this applicant, "A gawky, nice lad, unimpressive on all counts. I warned him he would have to make a lot of progress if he is to qualify. I'm rooting for him!" The boy's average was only 72.3, though both of his aptitude scores were higher than Carlson's. His headmaster wrote, "A pleasant, friendly person as you come to know him. He is quiet and retiring, serious and practical, with little imagination. He is a plugger and will never set the world on fire. But he will work and keep on trying even if things are not too easy for him. He has his own kind of dignity, as well as something soft and somewhat young for his age. You will often see in his face a sensitivity, a sweetness, a moodiness, and a certain potential strength. I am certain he will grow to a fine, sympathetic manhood. He is coming up fairly quickly this year."

"The main thing about this chap," Thompson said after examining the boy's senior grades, "is that he *is* coming up. You can be sure he will not get in unless he can do the work. The sort of pressure on Howe that this folder represents is fairly routine. You'd be surprised at the eminent people whose boys are turned down. Apparently it's just about impossible for brilliant fathers to realize that the chances of their sons being equally brilliant are very small. I have the greatest respect for Howe. He stands his ground."

Now Thompson began shuffling through the folders I had not yet read, to see if there were any that might illustrate other special problems. In a few minutes, he opened one, and I saw from the attached photograph that it was that of a handsome Negro youth. "Here's part of the price we pay for our academic standards," Thompson said. The boy, whom I'll call Bob, came from a highly industrialized Eastern city and was applying for a scholarship. He reported that he could contribute only a hundred dollars from his summer earnings, because the rest had to go to his family, whose total income was thirty-eight hundred dollars a year. "This boy's parental guidance has been intellectually and morally far from what one would consider desirable," the alumni interviewer wrote. "His parents are almost illiterate—his father an unemployed invalid and his mother a laundry worker. Both his younger brothers dropped out of school in the eighth grade, one because of asthma and the other because of heart trouble. Bob has had remarkable success in both scholarship and athletics. He is No. 1 in his class of 500, and has had a straight A average since the seventh grade. He is the first Negro president of the Student Council, and is also the varsity quarterback and captain of the No. 2 basketball team in the state. I am impressed with his sensitivity, alertness, and modesty. His record has so impressed his own race that the area's leading Negroes are guaranteeing five hundred dollars a year toward his college expenses." The initial excitement of the Yale staff over Bob's candidacy was clearly evidenced by the documents in the folder. Then the boy's College Board scores had begun coming in. In the aptitude tests, he had averaged only 488, and in his achievement tests he had scored 398 in English, 437 in social studies, and 474 in physics. The last papers in the file were a letter to his school's principal from Howe and the principal's reply. Usually, Howe wrote, in the case of a disparity between school record and test scores, Yale gives greater weight to the school record, but Bob's College Board results, if he were admitted, would certainly be the lowest in the entire Yale class. "Yale is prepared to give the necessary financial assistance," the letter went on. "This youngster seems clearly to represent the kind of leadership that his race critically needs. But certainly it would be a tragedy if he were to come to Yale and not be successful in meeting the requirements." Howe then asked the principal to tell him frankly whether he felt that Bob could do Yale work. The principal's letter obviously represented as much worried thought as Howe's. "I am now certain that Bob would be unable to do the work at Yale," he wrote. "Evidently he has worked to his greatest capacity here with us and has spent many long hours achieving his grades."

A little later we came across the folder of a lad who represented another part of the toll paid for high scholastic standards. He was a talented young musician who wanted to be a concert pianist and had already appeared in solo performances in New York City. Tuttle had described in detail his interview with him. The boy hoped to get a liberal arts degree and at the same time emerge from Yale ready for the concert stage. Could he handle both the academic work and five hours of practice on the piano a day, he wanted to know. Tuttle had taken him to the music school where the chairman told him that though there were a number of undergraduate performers at Yale who managed to practice three hours daily on the piano, five, in his opinion, would be impossible. At the end of the boy's folder was his reluctant letter of withdrawal from Yale, saying that he had decided instead to attend a professional music institution.

Before Thompson left I asked him if there were any pitfalls in selection that a scientist on the admissions board would be useful in helping to avoid. He replied that there were. "More boys apply to college today saying that they want to be scientists than was the case even five years ago. Quite a few of them find out later that they are really not cut out for the work. Along with their applications they often include detailed descriptions of some scientific project they've completed or some prize they've won. Some of these sound fairly advanced. The scientists on the committee can check their quality on the spot or phone around till he finds someone doing research in the same subject who can," he said. "Often the work turns out to be no more than fussing around with electronic gadgets. The boy's math and science grades may even be mediocre. There has to be a solid mental side to his interest or it's too often just little-boy tinkering."

Sometimes a youngster with scientific talent needs interpreting to committee members, Thompson continued. "He's often been hiding away, working and brooding either alone or with another kid like himself. He's apt to be gauche and untidy and socially unsure of himself, unlike the musician or the athlete, say, who have been working with other people and usually come off better in interviews. Our alumni interviewers may miss on these scientific chaps. The breath of fresh air the former bring us here in the ivory tower is good. But often they are businessmen who like boys who can meet them 'man to man'—and this predilection has to be taken into consideration. Frequently they write of one of these serious scientific youngsters, 'Seems to be lacking in personality,' or 'I couldn't get much out of him.' Yet he may be precisely the young scientist we want."

Howe had told me that I would find little or no difference in the quality of the boys rated A from the Eastern part of the country and those, say, from the far West, where Yale, along with other Ivy League colleges, is eager to find promising candidates and thus maintain its status of a national university. As I read along through the folders after Thompson had left, I made a check of the applicants with A ratings from a couple of top high schools in the New York City area and similar candidates in the West. I could find no indication that Yale's standards had been appreciably more lenient with the latter. The Eastern boys ranked B, however, seemed to have higher board scores, higher predictions, and more outstanding academic records than the B boys from other regions of the country. A corollary seemed to be that if Yale were to select its freshmen entirely from the East, the class would probably be of even higher academic promise than the present one resulting from selection on a national basis.

As the time for the committee meetings drew near, I found that I had become intensely interested in the fortunes of a number of boys—both A candidates and borderline cases. One boy whose fate I was curious about, but whose folder I had deliberately ignored, was a family friend I had known since he was a child; my guess was that he would not be admitted. Also among my dark-horse entries, in addition to Rodney Carlson, Ned Summers, and the son of the important alumnus, was a Puerto Rican boy, the eldest of five children, whose parents were on relief. He had spent the past two years on scholarship at a well-known prep school, whose headmaster, recommending him, wrote, "He has had to come all the way on his own, and the way has been long. His strength lies well below the surface, as he has had little instruction in how to make a successful impression. As an undergraduate he will not be in a position to realize his potentialities, because he is still working to catch up, but his potentialities are great, and will, I am confident, be realized before many years following graduation." His prediction figure, I noticed, was only 62.

Another doubtful case I found myself concerned about was that of a stocky, rather troubled-looking youngster, whom I will call Joseph Simon, from a high school near Boston. His guidance man wrote that he was recommending Simon for Yale, though by doing so there was some danger of his losing his annual wager of a beer with Howe over his predictions as to his candidates' successful work at the college. The boy was a varsity athlete, though not of college calibre. He was ranked three by his school for both personal and academic promise and four by Yale. His math aptitude score was 800 and his English 765, but his achievement marks were in the low 600's and 700's. "Joseph has been his own worst enemy," wrote the counselor. "His weakness is an immaturity which he is both rapidly outgrowing and trying to overcome. He continues to show up at his worst in the face of frustration. But he has finally learned not to be impatient with boys who think more slowly than he does, and is becoming liked by his classmates for the first time in his life. The foregoing minuses in my opinion are far outweighed by his ability. He will handle college courses with distinction if he wants to, and I believe he will." The Yale interviewer commented: "Unless I am completely crazy this is a really first-rate lad. If reports continue favorable we should probably move him from B to A status." His rating, however, had not been changed and I was anxious to see how he would fare with the committee itself.

The last boy whose fortunes I'd become interested in I'll call Grant Todd. Howe had handed me his folder one morning with a glint in his eye. Grant's case was well summed up by the alumni interviewer's report: "This lad comes from an outlying county in one of the less populous Northwestern states. He has a rugged, strong face. He's awkward, odd, homely, and shy, and has a most unusual inner self-determination. His background is the most important thing about him. His father runs a small dry farm—a subsistence proposition—and there are three younger sons. His mother once taught school up in the mountains. They have one mule, a 1950 pickup Chevy, no debts, and eleven hundred dollars in the bank to buy seed, etc., for their next year's wheat crop. Their income varies from twenty-six to thirty-one hundred dollars, and they offer two hundred out of it, plus the entire five hundred Grant has saved from summer jobs. Grant is the top student in his high-school class of a hundred, popular and respected and good at baseball and basketball. His principal speaks of his 'superb reliability' and his 'stabilizing influence.' The school has a limited curriculum (no foreign languages) and has never had a graduate go out of state to college. His counselor is as much surprised as I am at Todd's application. Neither of us is able to find out where he got the idea of Yale. He just says quietly he is determined to get a liberal education and then study law at Yale. He has never been out of his community, and when I pointed out what a big step this would be, he was unimpressed. I rank him near the very top—2—as an individual. As a scholar I can make no recommendation at all." Plainly, Yale was similarly stumped. "Would we kill him if we took him?" queried one admissions-committee reader. Burnham had taken a deep plunge and came up with a shaky prediction figure of 79. The next thing I found in Grant's file was a letter from Howe to one of the country's best preparatory schools, saying that Grant "comes awfully close to epitomizing the kind of talented youngster we all talk about and do very little about." Howe had proposed that the school take the boy on scholarship for the last half of his senior year, and then for summer school. The final documents in the dossier were a report from the prep school, recommending Grant for Yale on the ground that he had been slowly forging ahead scholastically, and a report on his College Board aptitude and achievement scores, which ranged from 500 to 657.

CHAPTER

SEVEN

BY the first of April, two weeks before the committee was to begin its meetings, the tension about the admissions office was high. In the last stages of preparing the slate of candidates, Howe and his staff were now taking home large bundles of folders for reading every night and over the weekends. They were pondering difficult cases, adjudicating others, and checking grouping results. They were balancing individual scholarship needs against the total allotment of gifts, loans, and jobs available, as well as determining the type of scholarship to recommend for each applicant, whether a Yale National, a general university grant, an alumni contribution, or, in a few cases, a corporate award given by some organization which allows Yale to select the recipient. Johnston, the alumni secretary, was making last-minute surveys with alumni committees to be certain, in admissions lingo, what "freight" each group could be counted on to "pick up" for each "body." The administrative assistants, Mrs. Fairchild and Miss Shirley Eberth, were straining their staffs to post on the folders the last college-board achievement scores and the final prediction figures which bursary boys were bringing over from Burnham's office.

The first meeting of the admissions committee was on Friday, April 15, and when I entered Welch Hall that morning there came to me from the far end of the corridor the rumble of many voices and the smell of tobacco smoke. Although I would not be permitted to hear the group's deliberations on individual boys, Howe had said that I might sit in long enough to hear him review the over-all admissions situation for the year and to get an idea of how the committee works. He had already told me that the only university restrictions under which the group operates are those limiting the class size and those stipulating the amount of money available for scholarships, loans, and jobs, which this year would total approximately $370,000, to go to a quarter of the students accepted. (These figures do not, of course, include the eighty or so students who are beneficiaries of what the admissions men call "outside scholarships," such as National Merit awards, endowed by the Ford Foundation and other private groups and corporations; General Motors scholarships; and Naval R.O.T.C. scholarships.)

Miss Bonnardi led me into the committee room, a large chamber dominated by a long table, where the nine members of the committee already sat, their jackets off and their sleeves rolled up. At the head of the table was Howe, wearing a tense, anticipatory expression that made me think of a man who is about to start pushing uphill an enormous weight that must reach the top at a given instant—in this case, May 10, the deadline for notification of the applicants. If the Yale replies were not in the mail in time to reach candidates by that deadline, it was indeed possible that a considerable portion of the college's hoped-for freshman class would melt rapidly into the comforting arms of rival institutions. Before Howe lay the stacks of folders and work cards of the boys whose applications were likely to come up for consideration that day. To one side was a cardboard chart marked into geographical regions across the country, where the totals for admission, admission with aid, rejection, and the scholarship sums awarded each day were to be listed.

Below Howe sat the two men from his staff who were on the committee, Waldo Johnston and Ralph Burr (the Director of Financial Aids in the admissions office), and the six other members: Harold Whiteman, Jr., the Freshman Dean; Grant Robley, Associate Dean of the School of Engineering; Richard Carroll, Associate Dean of Yale College; Oswald Tippo, Eaton Professor of Botany; H. Bradford Westerfield, Assistant Professor of Political Science; and Richard R. Shank, Assistant Professor of Electrical Engineering. I sat down in one of a group of chairs across the room from the committee table. Nearby were various people from Howe's department who were not members of the committee but who had come prepared to furnish information on applicants when it was needed. By herself at a small table against one wall sat Miss Elliot, huddled over a list of the applicants and ready to mark down the action taken on each.

Howe opened the meeting with the announcement that the sessions would run from ten to five-thirty, six days a week, and from two to seven-thirty on Sunday, for approximately two weeks. After each day's meeting, he said, he and the staff would review the folders of the boys whose names were coming up the following day, taking particular note of those whose scholastic status might have changed, those whose A ratings seemed questionable, and those about whom there would probably be special discussion for some other reasons. He went on to tell the committee that the year's competition had been tougher than ever, with five hundred more candidates than in the previous year, and a great many more scholarship applicants. "We had a total of 4,760 fee-paid applicants," he announced. "A hundred or so have dropped out, and a couple of hundred more have not yet been rated, because their records are still incomplete. For admission without scholarship, we have a total of 2,437 applications, 910 of them rated A. For admission with scholarship, we have 1,957, and 721 of these have been rated A. In all, we have 1,631 A candidates, 249 Bs, and 2,514 Cs. As you can see, we've been tougher than ever in our markings this year. We've reappraised the candidates who would ordinarily come to the meeting as B's and dropped many of them down to C."

"How many of the A candidates have we given commitments to in the grouping process?" one committee member asked.

"Five hundred and fifteen," Howe replied. "And I think that, with only a few exceptions, they are all boys you will want to take, although we can count on matriculation of only about three-fourths of them. The exceptions may cause you some anguish. Unhappily they do not now stack up with the total competition as they seemed to earlier. But they are commitments, and we must stick by them. Among the total five hundred and fifteen, incidentally, we have so far given only about thirty-five scholarship commitments. So our task is to choose about six hundred boys to be admitted without scholarships and about four hundred with scholarships, to bring our total up to fifteen hundred."

In each scholarship case, Howe added, he would recommend to the committee an individual pattern of spending, usually including a loan beside an outright grant and a job credit. "When the meetings are over," he said, "Ralph Burr will hurry up to Cambridge to compare our scholarship awards with M.I.T. and the rest of the Ivy group meeting for the purpose. We do this in an attempt to eliminate competitive bidding between us." In total sums awarded, he said, there is little difference from college to college among the conferees, though the considerable variety in the pattern of loan, gift, and job given a candidate sometimes makes it difficult to bring the awards into line.

Howe then asked the board to consider a mimeographed analysis of this year's candidates which lay before them from Burnham's office. There were 1,753 boys, it stated, applying from schools about whose standards Yale was well-informed, and 2,253 boys from schools about which it had little or no experience. Burnham had been able to make predictions for 4,006 of the candidates. Forty-nine were predicted to make a freshman average between 90 and 95; 506 between 84 and 89; 717 between 80 and 83; 1,179 between 74 and 79; 671 between 70 and 73; and 884 below 70, including 29 below 50. I learned later that several times during the sessions, the committee questioned individual boys' prediction figures and asked Burnham to explain them.

On the table before each committee member lay two heavy volumes, each about three inches thick, into which had been compressed, in highly telegraphic form, essential data about each of the candidates. The books, which are arranged by geographical regions, by states within each region, and by schools within each state, list six or eight applicants per page, with four or five lines of hieroglyphics for each. The listings from New York State alone accounted for over one hundred pages. Opening the first volume, Howe translated, for the benefit of the committee members, one of the entries, which looked approximately as follows:

```
AS GREEN ARTHUR WILLIAM 34YC   J   1600   41
  2 SAN FRANCISCO CALIF      2354   81 1   83 7
  2 ARROW SCHOOL      ARROWSMITH CALIF
D 709      761
M          EN 763  SS 761  CH 664
```

This, Howe explained, described an A-rated boy who was applying for a scholarship ("S"), whose name I have changed to Arthur William Green, whose father was a 1934 graduate of Yale College, who was known to be a scholarship applicant at other institutions ("J" meaning "Joint Applicant"), who would require $1,600 in financial assistance, and who had himself been born in 1941. Green had been rated 2 for personal promise by an alumni interviewer in San Francisco and by his teachers at what I have called the Arrow School, in the nonexistent town of Arrowsmith, California. The "2354" meant that he had been rated 2 for personal promise by his school principal, 3 by one Yale reader, 5 by another, and 4 by still another. His School Grade Adjusted was 81, and his freshman prediction was 83. The "1" after the "81" meant that Burnham's office gave the highest possible rating to the scholastic standards of Green's school; the "7" after the "83" meant that the prediction was based on the fullest data possible. The fourth and fifth lines summed up Green's College Board tests: in December he had taken the aptitude exams and scored 709 in verbal skill and 761 in math, and in March he had taken the scholastic-achievement tests, scoring 763 in English, 761 in social studies, and 664 in chemistry.

Miss Elliot had promised to tell me when I must leave the meeting, and I glanced uneasily at her as the group went on to discuss Green in more detail, referring to the folder readers' comments on him, reading from interview reports and from his teachers' questionnaires, and analyzing his school grades. Then, as they began the same process with the next boy on the list, I realized that Howe was going through all of the candidates on one full page of the big book to refresh the minds of the committee members on the various rating methods. At the close of an exhaustive discussion of why one boy's high-school average had suddenly dropped (apparently because he had been made football captain) a slump which would have proved fatal had he been applying for a scholarship, Howe called for the voting to begin, and Miss Elliot hurried over and asked me to leave.

I saw very little of either her or Howe during the next two weeks, though I dropped in at the office fairly often. In the filing room, where I had done my folder reading, clerks and bursary boys dashed to and fro, putting away the dossiers on candidates who had already been voted upon and digging up those of the boys next in line, and occasionally a staff man hurried in from the committee room to search for the folder on a boy whose case had been reopened in the light of some decision on another candidate. The phones rang almost continuously. Many of the calls were from anxious principals and headmasters, and these were told that Howe would wire or phone them as soon as he had word on their students. Even more calls were from applicants. Often, after listening to an apparently breathless query from a boy, Miss Bonnardi or Mrs. Heywood would ask soothingly, "What college is raiding you?" The "raiders" were colleges that did not subscribe to the Candidates' Reply Date Agreement. They had already sent out their bids, and were now demanding immediate decisions. The anxious boys were told that their school heads should get in touch with Howe, who would wire them as soon as the cases had been decided. In one instance, though, when an Indiana boy called to report that he had only twenty-four hours before he must reply to a scholarship offer from Amherst, his folder was rushed right into the committee, and soon Moll, the Hoosier enthusiast, emerged to dictate a wire to Miss Bonnardi. Moll's message, which Miss Bonnardi later told me she had discreetly edited a bit, was "Damn Amherst. Definitely accepted. On aid requested chances good but not final. Hold fast." A few conscientious school directors called to report sadly that theretofore promising boys who had already passed the board, had failed courses or had had to be expelled because of sudden disciplinary disasters, and a few people—educators or parents—called to make outright appeals that certain boys be accepted. (None of these pleas, I was told, were as insistent as one a few years ago from a United States ambassador, who not only called from his foreign post to demand that a particular boy be taken but later the same day had his secretary call back to make sure Yale realized that it had indeed been His Excellency who had phoned.) On one occasion, Mrs. Heywood dashed in to Howe with a special-delivery letter that, he later told me, came from a father whose income had just been drastically reduced and who was worried about whether he could still afford to send his son to Yale. The committee made an appropriate increase in the aid given the boy.

At the end of four days the committee had completed action on the candidates for Yale from Hawaii, Alaska, and the far Western region of the country, as well as from the Rocky Mountain, North-central, and South-central areas. Of the 957 candidates it had considered, it had admitted 274, and had voted scholarships, adjusted in each case to individual financial needs, to 131 boys. It had put fifty-one students on the reserve list where they stood a chance of admittance if enough higher-ranking candidates decided to go elsewhere. The high proportion of scholarships awarded in the group was due to the fact that in those geographical areas a large portion of the candidates needed financial assistance. On some days, I learned from one of the staff men, a lot of territory was covered by the committee, while on others things ground to a halt for what my informant called "one of our glorious fights." Among them had been several over how far the committee should go in favoring legacies, a subject into which I later got some insight from an administrator of one of the better preparatory schools. The latter's grading system was only a few points more lenient than Yale's. Of the eight legacies admitted from this institution, seven had averages of from 75 to 77 at the school, while all of the nonlegacies had stood in the 80's except for one student averaging 79. The committee had also had a lengthy discussion over whether a fine boy and good student from a badly broken home could stand up under both the challenge of a full scholarship with its accompanying job, and the incessant emotional demands his family put upon him. As the lad wanted to become an engineer, his school record was given a particularly careful scrutiny by the representatives from that department on the board before he was approved. Another prolonged disagreement had arisen over the candidacy of a boy from a small fundamentalist religious sect known for its rigid customs and outlook. Debate went on for an hour and a half over whether the youngster could adjust to Yale without a profound shock to his equilibrium. He was finally accepted. Action by majority vote was resorted to in the usual one out of every five or six cases considered, and Howe, as chairman, had already stepped in to resolve one of the two dozen or so tie votes apt to be encountered during the two weeks of meetings.

"These committee people aren't yes men," Miss Elliot remarked to me during a break. "They ask a huge number of questions, and they continually challenge university policy. Each year it's announced that there is little or no point in reviewing all the records of the boys rated A, but each year they are gone over. The Bs get very intensive reconsideration, and even the Cs aren't a closed book, by any means. Every case on which the staff readers have disagreed becomes a long-drawn-out affair, as most of the contents of the folder are read aloud. That's what is done with other problem cases, too. The prodigal sons always get the attention, don't they?"

When the committee adjourned, on May 2nd, it had definitely admitted 1,609 boys, put 289 more on a reserve list to await possible vacancies, and delegated to Howe and his staff the unenviable task of deciding which hundred boys would have to be taken off the admissions list. After two days and nights of furious work in Welch Hall, the final list was ready to go to the clerical staff, which sorted the bids and rejections for mailing, so that—theoretically, at least—they would arrive everywhere in the country on Tuesday, May 10. Every principal or headmaster whose school had Yale applicants was sent a notice telling him how all his boys had come out. To every successful candidate went a form notice with a request for an early decision on Yale's bid, and a request for a non-refundable fifty-dollar registration deposit against his future expenses. All the boys who had not made it were sent letters signed by Howe, who saw to it that those among them whose fathers happened to be alumni were not notified until the news had been broken, also in letters from him, to the old grads.

Almost immediately Yale students began besieging Miss Bonnardi to find out if brothers or friends had been admitted, and the accepted boys themselves to flood the office with their replies, some making excited calls to the staff men who had interviewed them, others sending scribbled letters and cards. "May I extend my sincere thanks for your invitation?" wrote one boy, while another, who had been rejected, took it like a man, to the extent of thanking the staff "for all the consideration it has given my application," and adding, "I know it is a tremendous task to consider and choose a student body." One Southerner wrote, "I am overjoyed and gratified to learn of my acceptance at Yale, but an unexpected consideration compels me to accept Harvard instead. My mother would like you to please add the enclosed hundred-dollar check toward the education of some needy boy from our state, as she says she will always have a soft spot in her heart for Yale."

Another student rejected an $1800 scholarship. He had decided to attend instead a small community college in his home town, thereby saving his parents $300 a year. "That is the kind of decision that really makes us sad," commented a staff member.

CHAPTER
EIGHT

A COUPLE of weeks after the admissions meetings had ended, I made my final visit to Welch Hall, and found it restored to comparative calm. On my way in to see Howe, who had promised to tell me how the boys whose candidacies I was following had made out, I met Moll, who paused for a chat. He told me that three youngsters were still gnawing their fingernails and trying to decide between other colleges and Yale, which had given them a few more days to make up their minds. The Indiana boy who had been raided by Amherst had decided on Yale, he added, but the crippled artist had been turned down, solely because the special attendant he needed would have had to occupy space in a dormitory, and there was no space left. The boy whose father had tried to bribe Moll with his services had been rejected. "We couldn't help wondering how far he had absorbed his father's standards," said Moll. "And there were too many applicants with qualifications as good as his who didn't have that question mark after them." Moll had won an office pool whose object was to come closest to guessing the number of boys who would have sent in their acceptances by May 18th—in this case, nine hundred and six. "And, finally," Moll said, "the Freshman Dean's office is already telling us that the incoming class is the brightest ever."

I found Howe looking considerably more relaxed than when I had last seen him. I congratulated him on the number of acceptances and on the brightness of the class, and he thanked me soberly. "I wish I could feel more elated," he said. "But the trouble is that you so often know you have turned down boys who are just as promising as the ones you've taken. You don't know why. It just turns out that way." He went on to read me part of a letter, from that morning's mail, in which a mother begged to be told why her son had been rejected when boys with lower test scores and school averages had been taken. Her son, she said, was completely discouraged. "Unless we can help him by giving him a good reason for his rejection, I am afraid he will not try again to give his best to his studies."

"Her son's a good boy," Howe said, leafing slowly through the youngster's folder, which lay on his desk. "He could probably do work in the high 70s here. Well, I could write a book to this woman." Howe also had the folder of the boy I knew, who I had been sure would be rejected. "That friend of yours was admitted," he said, "and on not as good a record, or such high exam scores. We just thought he was more of a guy than this lady's son. Your friend isn't much of a scholar. In fact, as far as schoolwork goes he's mediocre in comparison with many others, though he has a fine brain. But his guidance man summed it up pretty well when he called him 'a sensitive, intelligent force for good.' Well, we turned down boys doing honors work in order to accept him, and that's our answer to people who say we don't take chances on the slow developers."

I learned that Rodney Carlson had been rejected but that the athletic department was fairly happy anyway, since the accepted candidates included the football guard who liked

French poetry, the freckled three-letter man, a quarterback whose College Board average was over 750, and a couple of sprinters with predictions for honors work. The committee had turned down another fine athlete, however, only to learn that he had been given a scholarship by what a staff member called "Yale's most intellectual rival." Joseph Simon, the B-rated youngster with the high test scores whose guidance man was betting a beer on him, had been admitted by the committee after evidence that he had suddenly burst into bloom with a series of academic and personal accomplishments. The important benefactor's son had been rejected, the Puerto Rican boy had been accepted, and Ned Summers, the inarticulate youngster with the high test scores, about whom Thompson had been apprehensive, had been put on the reserve list (but, I've since learned, ultimately didn't get in). Grant Todd, the determined Northwestern boy from the subsistence farm, was definitely a member of the new freshman class. When I indicated my pleasure at this, Howe gave me a stern look. "The boy whose mother wrote to us is abler than Grant Todd. Sometimes I think there's a peculiar form of self-justification in our decisions. I guess we're trying, in the words of the original Yale charter, to serve 'Church and Civil State.' But the sad fact is that two or three of every ten such long-shot chances we take just don't work out."

Now, Howe went on, the admissions staff was looking ahead to next year. "The atmosphere was pretty thick around here after the lists went out," he said. "Disappointed people rang our phones for days, and there was a line of parents practically with bullwhips out in the anteroom. I don't see how we can endure another year like it. We won't sacrifice the thoroughness with which we consider each candidate, so we're making some changes. To give ourselves a little more time, we're advancing to December the deadlines both for applications and for all of the College Board exams (we're reducing the achievement tests to two). And to help us further in evaluating the boys we've decided to ask for, of all things, an additional test—and an essay test at that. It will be given by the College Board people, but read by us. The boys will simply be asked to write for an hour on some such subject as 'The Most Meaningful Experience of My Life.' We think the results will give us some insights we don't at present get into their ability to organize their thoughts and to set them down, as well as into their characters."

Just before I left, Howe said, "If there's any real skill in this work, it's probably in shaping the over-all composition of the class—in working out what seems to be a balanced design. But if you want to know how difficult it is, come up here in September and sit on the fence out on the Old Campus and watch these kids arriving, with all their hopes and fears in their faces, and all their parents' hopes and fears right behind them—not to mention ours. Then ask yourself which ones will make good and which ones won't."